I have arrived before my words

I HAVE ARRIVED BEFORE MY WORDS

AUTOBIOGRAPHICAL

WRITINGS OF

HOMELESS WOMEN

Deborah Pugh and Jeanie Tietjen

CHARLES RIVER PRESS

Alexandria, Virginia

Published by
CHARLES RIVER PRESS
427 Old Town Court
Alexandria, Virginia 22314-3544
Design by Bonnie Campbell

Cover: Doris Lee (American, 1905–1983), *Cherries in the Sun (Siesta),* ca. 1941. Oil on canvas, 27 × 36 in., The National Museum of Women in the Arts, Gift of The Honorable Clare Boothe Luce.

Grateful acknowledgment is made for permission to use an excerpt from Lucille Clifton's "what the mirror said." Copyright © 1978 by Lucille Clifton. Now published in *good woman: poems and a memoir 1969–1980* by BOA Editions, Ltd. Reprinted by permission of Curtis Brown, Ltd.

Library of Congress Cataloging-in-Publication Data
Pugh, Deborah.
    I have arrived before my words : autobiographical writings of homeless women / Deborah Pugh and Jeanie Tietjen.
        p.   cm.
    Includes bibliographical references and index.
    ISBN 0-9647124-2-3 (pbk.)
    1. Homeless persons' writings, American.
2. Homeless women—United States—Biography.
3. Autobiography—Women authors.
    I. Tietjen, Jeanie. II. Title.
    PS508.H65P84   1997
    818'.5080809206086942—dc20   96-43936
                                      CIP

Manufactured in the United States of America
10 9 8 7 6 5 4 3 2 1
Printed on recycled paper.

CONTENTS

PREFACE

Deborah Pugh and Jeanie Tietjen

This book is about women, autobiography, and our experiences teaching writing and literature in homeless shelters and jail. But more than that, it is about how seven women from different backgrounds, different races, and different circumstances came together to break silences and to learn from each other. This book tells one story composed of seven parts.

We first came together in fall 1994 as participants in WritersCorps —a collaboration between AmeriCorps, President Clinton's federally funded community service program, and the National Endowment for the Arts. WritersCorps, which is also supported by local cultural agencies in three cities, is an arts-in-service project that employs writers as teachers in communities traditionally underserved by the arts. Poets and writers from diverse backgrounds lead workshops among the homeless, at-risk youth, senior citizens, incarcerated women and men, substance abusers, children and adults living with mental illness, women and children in temporary shelters from domestic violence, and in many other community centers. Writing workshops are conducted in the Bronx and San Francisco, as well as in our location, Washington, D.C. The writers who teach in the program are working artists of many ages and interests who share a commitment to community service. WritersCorps gives them a small stipend and educational benefits for a maximum of two years service.

The seven of us whom you'll meet in these pages are testimony to what such programs as WritersCorps can do to tear down barriers and improve lives. We two teachers are white, college-educated women who chose to work at minimum-wage jobs because that lifestyle allowed us the personal freedom and necessary time to develop as writers. A network of support, including family and friends, acts as a balancing agent, keeping us from the isolation low income can often effect. Jeanie was in her late twenties when she entered the program, and Debbie was forty.

Our five students (who became our teachers too) are five women who are or have been homeless. They range in age from their twenties to their fifties. Four of them are black, one is white; two have drug problems; two have been in prison; three are mothers; one has been in the military; two have problems with mental illness; one is disabled; four were victims of sexual abuse as children or young women; one is currently enrolled in college, and two others have some college education. They have been marginalized because of their gender, their class, their behavior, their physical, mental, and emotional challenges—yet each is a citizen of our country, a part of our society, a voice deserving to be heard.

Other books chart, document, and analyze the social and cultural phenomena these women experience. Through the pages of this book, we want you to know these women for themselves—to see how different they are from each other, to see what interesting writers they are, to see how they got to be where they are and where they're going. Autobiographical writing is ideal for this purpose, for it insists on the primacy of the individual: it puts the person before the problem. In doing so, it functions to emphasize the value and uniqueness of that one individual.

The first section consists of our first-person narratives. We give you glimpses into our ideas and life experiences and what brought us, as women and writers, to this program.

The second section contains the autobiographical writings of five currently or formerly homeless women—Gayle, Ann, Georgia, Dionne, and Angie. While the issues they face and the lives they lead are similar to those of many other homeless women, they should in no sense be considered representative. In fact, we chose these five from the many with whom we worked because of the diversity of their experiences and writing styles, as well as because of the special connections we felt with them. These women are very different types of writers, incorporating genres ranging from folk tale to confession, from poetry to science fiction, from tragedy to comedy, from family history to myth. All include some aspect of a traditional quest narrative: they seek self-expression, self-knowledge, and a physical and emotional place where they belong. Some of them have reached extraordinary levels of insight into their own past, their families, and themselves; others idealize or mythologize those elements, show unresolved conflicts about them, or do not deal with them at all.

We worked with these five women to write their own stories and then to organize and edit their writing. We encouraged the women (sometimes successfully) to expand on parts of what they had written. We also agreed to omit parts they did not want published and to change some names. In preparing the manuscript for publication, our editor lightly copyedited their selections, but only to the extent of regularizing spelling or punctuation or cutting a word or phrase here or there to improve the flow of the narrative. In no way did any of us write these women's stories or put words into their mouths.

Following each woman's autobiographical narrative is a discussion written by either Jeanie or Debbie. In these discussions, we provide additional information about each woman and suggest some of the many possible ways to analyze her writing. Our suggestions are certainly not the only way to read their work; our discussions are merely our individual perspectives on these women's stories and how the decisions they make as writers reflect their experiences and personalities.

All of us, of course, including these women, swap stories for many reasons: a desire to vindicate or explain, to vent anger, despair, or frustration, to entertain, to gain acceptance, to give allegiance or withhold it, to open ourselves to or hide from the listener. In telling a story, we must bring the chaos of existence to the table of interpretation in order to extract the meaning of experience. And the interaction of listening and responding in story enables us to make understandable and meaningful contact with other human beings.

As storytellers and writers, we believe that our lives and the lives of all people are touched and even transformed by story. For too many years, decades, centuries, the proper voice for women has been one of silence. But the power to speak one's experience is the beginning of the power to change one's world. From this book, you will see the female universality of autobiography, for it is about joy, courage, creativity, hope, triumph, failure, family, love, death, and desire. It is about life lived with labels and expectations and, in some cases, beyond them.

This is a book about writing, but after you turn the last page, we hope you will realize it is also a book about love. We seven women wanted to give something of ourselves to each other, so we combined our talents and will share the rewards and royalties that result. Our experience together disproves the notion that people must be hopelessly polarized if they do not share a social or educational background, a standard of living, a racial or ethnic identity. Rather, it shows that well-intentioned individuals can cross all those boundaries and can do so whether they are living in homes or living homeless.

It is our hope that you will take something away from this book as well—something that will help you speak out and change your life. We hope that you will also come away, as we have, with renewed respect for how language and literature accompany us even in our most intimate journeys—making experiences our own, bringing us finally some fulfillment of home.

Two Women Teaching, Writing, Learning

ONE

WRITING HOME

Jeanie Tietjen

I am a writer who teaches with other writers in this nation's capital, proclaiming the process of writing as a valuable endeavor. To my surprise, we have been proven correct in our assertion that writing transforms and heals. That my students are homeless or poor or incarcerated or suffering from debilitating mental and/or physical illness is not my primary concern. These realities are hardly minor: in fact, they loom, dictate, and restrict. But I am that dogged, persistent voice of the muse, saying, "Well, yes, you have experienced this, and what do you have to say about it? How can you describe it? How have other writers in similar situations approached this subject?"

My approach to teaching is derived from an American intellectual history course I took at the University of Washington in Seattle in the mid-1980s. The instructor was clean-shaven and wore a bow tie and unglamorous spectacles. Before each class, he would remove his jacket, stand behind the podium in front of the chalkboard, occasionally wiping his forehead with a handkerchief, and wait silently for the bell to signal the start of class. In a no-nonsense tone he announced that, in spite of the diversity of academic concentrations in the room, during the daily meetings of this class and in each essay and term paper he expected us to conduct ourselves as historians. This standard terrified the nonhistorians like me and in all likelihood gave pause to some majoring in the field, but we consequently discovered we had no choice but to succeed as historians. The instructor's exacting requirement transformed the process of learning and our expectations of ourselves. His refusal to disqualify us on the basis of who we were created new possibilities.

I heartily emulate this instructor's approach in each class I teach and every workshop I lead. My students are writers first; that is my mandate and belief. This one received a masters in social work more than a decade ago, before the onset of hallucinations and the selfmedication of alcohol. This one had her first child at sixteen and never graduated from high school. This one is addicted to crack cocaine. This one, born and raised in Ethiopia, now lives far from home on the streets of Washington. This one was raised right here in the city, but her family cannot tolerate her love for other women. This one was married to a man who beat her for twenty years, divorced her when the kids were grown, and forgets alimony while she struggles to learn WordPerfect. This one is homeless; lives in low-income housing; has temporary residence with a friend or relative. Each one is a writer.

WHAT I AM as a writer and teacher of writing emerges out of my own past experiences of home. I was born in Northern California and spent my early childhood, literally, in Paradise. My father, a Lutheran minister, had his first parish in this small community of mostly retired folks far away from the California-dreaming land of beaches and stars and palm trees. Our family lived in a small parsonage and ate vegetables from our garden. Sometimes my older brother and I went with my dad to call on church members, riding long distances in the car through the red earth and tall pines, across flat, hot fields.

My parents, married thirty-odd years now, are not wealthy, but they have devoted their lives to providing rich structure and opportunity for their children. I am lucky because I am loved for who I am. I am also lucky because I've always seen the written word as something magical, whether appearing in street signs, billboards, cereal boxes, hymns, or books—especially books, and especially after my kindergarten teacher gave me *Where the Wild Things Are*. This acclaimed illustrated book by Maurice Sendak follows a young boy, Max, one night when he is sent to bed and the walls in his room give way to a wild jungle. The fiction of this great adventure never seemed implausible to me. In fact, reading created a wildness in my own mind, allowing what I imagined to become possible. I was never able to get the parsonage to buckle under the night sky, but I believed I could compel our cat to come to me through force of mind, make a horse appear in the garden, or send the school rug flying over the trees with my brother and me piloting the tassels.

When my father accepted another call, the family moved to Cincinnati, Ohio. During that period, I remember watching him with other young scholars in their clerical collars, sitting around our long dinner table with its red and white checked tablecloth and debating the future of the church, its relation to social change, and the ultimate relevance of the Bible to pressing questions of the time. I have since learned that their discussion concerned an ideological split in the Lutheran church, but at the time I heard only the intensity and camaraderie of their words. Conversation, it seemed, was the element of connection.

Around that same table at dinner nearly each night, our parents instructed us children to "look it up" if we didn't understand a word or concept. Their directive was not a dismissive gesture, but a challenge: if we were to understand, we had to discover through our own effort.

As I grew, my relationship with language changed when old words diminished against the pressure of experience. Imagination had once woven me into the world; but in my teen years, this interior world dissociated from the conscious life as things happened beyond my control or imagination. Books validated the existence of an interior world at odds with the actual. While the hallmark confusion of adolescence powered the interior world, literature provided a community of character and image to describe the sudden, powerful alienation. Experiences and impressions that outpaced my ability to comprehend were kept silent. I'd venture that each reader has a particular day or season or face wrapped carefully in a mantle of quietness. These are strong silences. We make room for them.

Around age seventeen, I began to move. I hitchhiked around my hometown, wandering unfamiliar streets, visiting the library, sometimes skipping school. I read books and magazines that transported me out of the city, out of the country. Movement, whether actual or imagined, soothed me. It eased the insistence to examine, kept the memories in proper order, directed the mind's eye with new ideas and people and places, held at bay flashes of what I could not understand. Moving forced the moment into the forefront, insisting on instinct over reflection.

Words betray me, however, when I say I have felt homeless or exiled. Placing myself in that group diminishes the meaning of the words and, by extension, the experiences of those cast out for reason of war, poverty, or prejudice. Unlike them, I have always departed willfully, with visions of green grass and some mysterious something I could not possibly know while standing still. The urgency of movement was not all compelled by sadness and confusion, but I know that my own form of exile—hiding from secrets inside myself—formed an unspoken yearning for the road. I have crossed and crossed again this country, sleeping in rest stops and cheap hotels. I've met nearly every specter of the highway and have, through sheer luck and the grace of good companions, survived to judge every inch of road precious. Occasionally, in the middle of the night at a bus stop in rural America, on a train rushing across eastern Europe, or hitching the freeway from Montreal to Toronto, the interior world would bleed out. I could go home at any point, and sometimes did. But because I ran from essential parts of myself, I felt homeless, estranged, never at peace.

I have written most of my life in response to this sense of homelessness. It's a very particular kind of mystery, where deep silences are knotted around alert, sensual people and places. The pressure between what has happened and what I can comprehend is a friction which, I suspect, will forever cross wires. Poet William Butler

Yeats describes this balancing magnetism as the "pressure inside" responding to the force from without. I map it: what I remember and what I desire form a very particular inner geography. A sheet of rain can be a vocabulary. The smell of a cigarette can reach into a pocket of fourteen years ago. What was once running has become writing. How much is coincidence and how much we cause through deliberation remain a matter of debate; but that I came to work as a writer with women experiencing all levels of actual homelessness is perhaps not so accidental as it seemed when I first began.

HOME IS A symbol for belonging, for connection with family—a shield against the chaos of the outside world. Photographs of those displaced from their homes reveal faces wiped with exhaustion and despair from Sarajevo to Rwanda to Cambodia. Refugee camps shelter survivors of our time's war and famine, but they cannot restore the village or neighborhood. Home is the symbol for security and warmth; its very mention suggests belonging—as in "I feel at home here." The pursuit of home or homeland has propelled human thought and action even in history's darkest moments. Testimonies bear witness not only to the devastation of Nazi Germany and Stalinist Russia, but to life before the Second World War, to the shtetls of eastern European Jews, to the neighborhoods of Vienna, Budapest, Prague. African-American culture endeavors to reconcile the two worlds of its people: Africa, the Motherland, the cradle of civilization, and America, the New World, for all its complexity and bitter history, home. It is as if to make a new and meaningful place as survivor, as refugee, one must remember, indeed re-create, the place one first called home.

For a short time in nineteenth-century France, homesickness was considered a pathology, a disease that could be remedied. Victims were young men who left their country villages for the military or to seek their fortunes in Paris. Young children removed from their nannies were also at risk for this affliction, displaying clear depressive symptoms that interfered, possibly fatally, with day-to-day functioning. Jean-Baptiste-Felix Descuret, a medical doctor, believed that nostalgia was essentially a psychological oppression, a freezing of the heart's memory in one point of the past. Effective remedies encouraged healing through intimate involvement with that thing the patient remembered and to which the malady was profoundly attached. The root of the word "nostalgia" is *nostos*, which means "home," and *algia*, which means "pain"—thus, "homepain." Aside from a longing for the past, nostalgia means sick for home or, as we have come to say, homesick. It is a cruel paradox of human nature that those who are currently homeless or refugees carry a longing for home, for a sense of belonging, perhaps more keenly than any others.

Land of the free, home of the brave is our nation's proud anthem, but except for Native Americans, all of us are immigrants. Our collective history on this continent has been shaped by movement: some of us came willingly, seeking new opportunities and freedom from poverty or religious persecution. Some of us were brought here as slaves, driving a stain into the psyche of our nation and profoundly altering all of us with its legacy of racism. Yet fundamental injustices have crippled the complete and just expression of constitutionally guaranteed rights from the earliest years of this democratic nation. Writer James Baldwin once said that the pain that signals a toothache is the pain that will save your life, and so it seems to me if we are "pained" by the sight of a woman sleeping day and night in a park near the White House, it is precisely that pain which indicates action.

In a society that esteems the endless varieties of individual achievement if only one works hard and tugs determinedly at the bootstraps, those who slip outside the customary measure of success are deeply unsettling. In New York City, hundreds of women and men live in tunnels beneath Manhattan; in Seattle and Portland, runaways and drifters construct shantytowns under bridges and near railyards; in parks and wilderness areas, old station wagons, tents, and trailers are home, sweet home; abandoned buildings, shutdown factories wrapped with wire, open campfires extend across this First World, these United States. According to a 1993 report from the National Law Center on Homelessness and Poverty, ten to fifteen thousand people are homeless on any given night in the District of Columbia, and 17 percent of the District's population lives in poverty. Statistics are a limited and flawed measure of the scope of homelessness in America, but here are some national figures from a 1995 report on hunger and homelessness. Single women comprise 14 percent of homeless persons, children 25 percent, and families with children (one parent and at least one child) 39 percent. Fifty-six percent are African-American, 29 percent white, 12 percent Hispanic, 2 percent Native American, and 1 percent Asian. Twenty-three percent of our nation's homeless are mentally ill, 46 percent are substance abusers, 8 percent are HIV-positive or have AIDS, 20 percent work full- or part-time, and 21 percent are veterans.

Some have the notion that all these women and men are somehow different—that by virtue of event or character or some mysterious disaster, they have suffered a profound tragedy that has transported them into a way of life utterly alien to those of us living in homes. The evening news documents displaced persons, telling us children are homeless in increasing numbers. Politicians sniff electoral winds to determine whether it is more or less advantageous to legislate funding for the poor and homeless. The frustration intensifies, the confusion grows: Do I give that woman outside the 7-Eleven fifty cents? Is she really that different from me? What is her story?

Because the correlation between ignorance and pain has been borne out so vividly in the twentieth century, it is on that very point that language concentrates its transformative possibilities. As literary critic and scholar Terrence Des Pres avows in *Writing into the World: Essays, 1973–1987* (1991):

Between the self and the terrible world comes poetry with its minute redemptions, its lyrical insurgencies, its willing suspension of disbelief in tomorrow. . . . What I mean to say is that right language can help us, as it always helps in hard moments, with our private struggles to keep whole, can be a stay against confusion, can start the healing fountains. And whatever helps us repossess our humanity, able again to take place and speak forth, frees us for work in the world.

What Des Pres so beautifully describes is what we call the language of witness. This is the world of literature spun from even the bleakest chapters of human history—the Holocaust, mass killings in Cambodia, brutal dictatorships, terrorism, and abuse. It speaks for the human spirit and its desire for wholeness, decency, an identity against the destruction, belonging, a home.

I HAVE SPENT nearly two years with my students. We study Shakespeare and the Psalms of King David, Nikki Giovanni and Lucille Clifton, Shaker feminist mystics from early America and Hungarian poets crying out from a death march across shattered Europe. But my classrooms are not at a school or college; they are at a drop-in center for homeless women and a correctional facility for incarcerated women. There is no standard age or education or reading level, no homework, no term papers, and no grading system. From nearly each text, with its variance in theme and temper, we read and we write.

That it happens at all is certainly at odds with the world beyond the classroom, which seeks, more often than not, to reduce all identity and possibility to a common denominator. Homeless woman. Incarcerated woman. Drug addict. Crazy bag lady. No one can say that the possibilities the imagination builds and the communion of telling one's own story in a supportive environment can heal poverty and mental illness and the damage sexual violence causes, nor does it alone combat the numbing call of substance abuse—but it does witness these nightmares. Telling one's own story reclaims the individual from the marginalization and anonymity these conditions engender. Telling one's story in nearly any environment, from the couch to the confessional to the campfire, persists as a fundamental human desire.

Not every woman on the streets or in prison, just as not every woman in a home, discovers the ambition to examine, think, and dream in writing. To tell a story, yes, we all do this in one manner or another. But what sets the women in this book apart (and others not represented by their own words here) is what they do: they write. Writing is a way of becoming, of asserting one's identity in spite of, in direct resistance to, the vast evidence of despair.

Memories encode meaning: sharing memories, even if they are not sunny or complete, knits us together in a communion of shared experience. The deliberate act of forgetting is a kind of violence to the soul. The loss of memory cuts one loose from roots, and those who do not accord value to what they remember run moment to moment in a kind of willful amnesia born of pain and bound to despair. One formerly homeless woman wrote, while she was still living in shelters and on the streets, that memories retrieve a special place for her:

I remember the good old days when
life seemed so simple, full of joy and
gladness. Memories often take me away
from the modern-day madness.

In *The Stories We Are* (1995), a study of storytelling, William Lowell Randall posits that our experiences indicate ways in which we have consciously engaged with the world; he further argues that how we tell and construct relationships with these experiences has a powerful impact on our self-understanding and the unfolding life. Modern culture describes the unconscious nature with phrases like "self-esteem" and "being in touch with the inner child." Connection to this "essential nature" is fundamental to conscious action, in what we persist doing and what we refuse. The process of writing draws deeply from this inner and vital place.

I approached the WritersCorps program with these essential convictions about the power of language in my own life, but I was not at all sure if it was possible to communicate them to others. In 1994, I moved from New York to Washington to find out.

I arrived in the midst of the almost-incomprehensible heat of

Washington's summer months. The Potomac River threads around the District, wrapping each night and day in a damp blaze. Vendors fan themselves in tiny carts, feeding pretzels and hot dogs wrapped in foil to newlyweds from Indiana and businessmen from Peru. They offer five-dollar sunglasses, ten-dollar watches ("special price just for you!"), Redskins T-shirts, and Hoya hats. Leopard print scarves hang motionless in the thick, humid air while incense streams in Myrrh and Opal and NightQueen. A card table outside the Popeye's Fried Chicken is surrounded by young guys selling meticulously arranged homemade cassettes of the Go-Go music native to Washington.

Two churches share a corner here, and beyond that, the Martin Luther King Memorial Library, the National Museum of American Art, and Chinatown. Between the library and the First Congregational Church, clumps of unlikely flowers bloom in season amid concrete and a profusion of bottles and bodies and bags. Up two short steps, and two more yet, I push open the smeared glass door of the church building into the beginning of this story: a smell of floor wax and skin and a thousand perfumes from the city and the women and men who live on its streets.

The First Congregational Church hosts in its basement a breakfast for homeless people in the morning and the Dinner Program for Homeless Women in the afternoon and evening. Following the advice of the director of the program, Reverend Linda Kaufman, about establishing a creative writing workshop, my team teacher, Imani Tolliver, and I spent the first few weeks acquainting ourselves with the program and the women it serves. The doors to the main dining area open at 4:30. From this time until dinner is served at 6:30, Linda provides various services, from arranging legal and medical counsel to distributing toiletries to monitoring use of a telephone the women may use free of charge. She mediates any disputes while the kitchen crew, including homeless women who are training in food preparation and service, prepares the evening meal.

The basic mission of the dinner program is to provide a nutritious hot meal to women in need and to give any woman and her children shelter from the streets. Respect for others in language and behavior is the only real requirement the women must meet. Nearly two years after my first day, I am still amazed that, given the tremendous diversity of personality among the women, I have not yet seen any serious threat to this environment. Linda certainly deserves credit for keeping the peace when conflict does occur, but there is a subtler, no less powerful force that originates in her constant attention to the women as individuals. The philosophy guiding her is posted on the wall above her desk: "If you've come to help me, don't waste your time. If you have come because your liberation is bound up in mine, then we can work together." This belief precludes any sentimental motivations behind service because it insists on the essential equality of provider and recipient. It is, in the words of Alexis de Tocqueville, "self-interest rightly understood." In *Democracy in America* (1835), de Tocqueville, a French visitor to early America, expressed his enthusiasm for the American experiment in democracy precisely because it balanced individual destiny with community welfare:

> The American moralists do not profess that men ought to sacrifice themselves for their fellow creatures *because* it is noble to make such sacrifices, but they boldly aver that such sacrifices are as necessary to who imposes them upon himself as to him for whose sake they are made.

That Linda's liberation is bound to mine and to that of the women she serves undergirds each tube of toothpaste she distributes, every bingo call, each greeting, and every frustration, creating an environment of respect most of the world outside does not share.

In my first days at the dinner program, I made flyers, set out some donated books, and sort of hoped the thing would come together. During announcements, Linda introduced me to the community several times, encouraging interested individuals to come and chat. A few women approached me, asserting they had books up here—tapping their foreheads—volumes of poetry in want only of a publisher. Very few of these women participated in the workshop, and I can only assume that their writings, wherever they exist, are worthy of some larger audience. I spent one afternoon, then another and another, sitting by myself behind this long table, arranging, rearranging, dusting, and counting the handful of books. I sat right next to the tea and juice spigots, smiling increasingly desperately as women filed by for beverages. A few kind souls feigned interest, perhaps feeling sorry for me. "Oh, honey," said one woman, "I hate to write, but I'm sure I'd come otherwise. Can I get you some juice?"

This was no Field of Dreams. The masses were not rallying in favor of a writing workshop simply by virtue of my presence. So Imani and I spent one Sunday afternoon devising an elaborate curriculum that examined nearly every genre of written expression. We wanted to leave no one out of our literary landscape. We created a chart that began with oral history and storytelling and moved into symbolist poetry, magical realism, and performance of the spoken word. This framework forced the surrender of a few trees in its creation, but it did little to advance the cause at the dinner program. I resumed my position at the table to shuffle and distribute, looking at the 75–100 faces with something approaching naked despair. This was the Works Progress Administration of the '90s, and I was personally responsible for its lackluster demise. But how could I reach these women? What could I say?

Finally, I got up, leaving the books and flyers and safe distance of the long table behind, and began introducing myself to individual women. Privacy is an elusive property for many homeless women because they sleep, eat, and pass many hours of the day surrounded on all sides by people in like circumstance. The women at the dinner program use the two hours before dinner to relax, read, listen to music through headphones, or simply sit without once being told to move. They invent a limited but potent privacy in this way. Many times I have sat on the steps and watched individual women create, through ritual, this space. One woman washes her hands first and then goes outside to smoke a cigarette. She returns to make herself a cup of coffee, tearing open sugar packets, stirring, blowing on the hot surface, then and only then, settling down into a chair for dinner. The rest of the day may consist of hustling, being hustled, or the constant crowding of close quarters, but this ritual invents a private world that, to this day, I hesitate to invade. Most of the women I approached, however, received me in good humor, and after a few weeks the workshop finally commenced. Four or five women attended regularly, forming the core class; many others participated less regularly.

The basement is large, and tables are set up in clusters across the floor. From 4:30 on, individual women arrive, pull a chair from the stack by the stage, and wait for dinner. Several tables of women play cards with a concentration and vigor I'd relish seeing any day in writing class. I've yet to conjure a consistently effective lure for the card players, though one of the class's finest prose writers lays out solitaire on the table where I find her nearly every afternoon. Her stories feature a detailed, rural landscape of childhood. She unfolds and sets observations in spare prose, one singular image following the other, with the same determination and pacing as in her card game. She's a white woman in her early to mid-forties. Small-boned, pale hair, blue eyes. I cannot say why she is homeless today any more than I can explain why she suddenly started leaving her cards, about once a week, in favor of writing. I hear occasionally of her frustrations, the weather, the overcrowding in the night shelters, the threat of theft when all one's possessions are carried in an unwieldy plastic bag. I'd be tempted to describe her as shy, except that she sometimes issues bold, incisive declarations in class, usually in response to work read aloud. Hers is an astute and sensitive voice, and I'll venture that this essential nature in such a clamorous world plays one small part in the life she now lives with such dignity, such grace.

At the dinner program, I learned quickly to dismantle stereotypes I harbored about homeless women. Many of the women, for instance, dress fashionably. If you stood next to them in line at a grocery store or museum, you would never guess they were homeless. In fact, a well-groomed appearance allows many of the women to blend into the community, to mingle at cosmetic counters, to read and study uninterrupted at libraries. Unless the weather is dramatically inclement, those who sleep in overnight shelters must be out on the streets by seven or eight a.m., not to return until much later that evening. For those women who are unemployed or not working that day, a multitude of hours open between the tightly constrained nights.

Care providers doubtless do the best job they can, but the women who spend nights in the trailers and, to a lesser degree, in shelters complain about theft and the habits of some of their bunk mates. I've heard countless stories about stolen property, threats of physical assault, poor personal hygiene, and rashes caused by infestation and disease. One of my students chose to sleep in city parks instead of shelters, preferring the outdoor risks of assault, rape, rats, and bad weather to the overcrowded trailers and church basements of winter months. The sheer exhaustion many of the women suffer intensifies other pressures: it shortens tempers, flattens motivation (and consequently, activity that might bolster self-esteem), and aggravates problems of physical and mental health. It initially unnerved me when a woman rocked herself and murmured quietly during class or another laughed aloud with no provocation—and I am by now thoroughly accustomed to varying levels of consciousness in the workshop. The ceaseless walking and walking, carrying all that one owns in bags and carts, taxes the body and thins resistance to hallucinations that drive many into the streets.

IN MY FIRST weeks, I spent time with women I have not seen again or glimpsed only rarely since. One such woman had her head wrapped in a sweatshirt. She was sitting quietly, winding and unwinding this shirt on her head with dirty fingers. She was small under all those layers and had a ring of hair around her mouth. But she was lucid, and we talked at some length. I described our writing workshop and encouraged her to attend. She and I chatted a bit more; then I closed by telling her my name and asking hers in return. She began stuttering where before she had been perfectly intelligible, and resumed the nervous raveling and unraveling of the shirtsleeves. I watched her perform incredible verbal acrobatics, hearing nothing cogent, until finally she stopped herself.

"To be honest," she said quietly, "it's been so long since someone asked my name that I can't remember. I can't remember my name."

The isolation this woman experiences is beyond loneliness. It is composed of a community's utter, completely accomplished rejection of her. Her visible destitution alienates her from many other homeless women as well, but it can paradoxically protect her on the streets. Sexual assault of homeless women, particularly those who live outside the shelter system, is commonplace. The disarray symptomatic of mental illness will *sometimes* repulse a would-be assailant. Rape and assault are, of course, expressions of hatred and violence, completely independent of standards of dress and all its associations, but extreme disintegration of the physical person can sometimes help render one invisible. Women from all over the world, and especially in wartime, have engaged in deliberate violation of the symbols of desirability to try and avoid rape and assault. Cutting the hair, dirtying the body, self-mutilation, and a host of other mechanisms have been employed as *conscious* tactics to discourage potential attackers.

But concealed deep within the wrappings is a woman given a name by her mother at birth, a woman who has a first and a last name and a hometown. This woman never came to class, but if she had, writing would demand one small thread of inner life. Words encode the intricacies and wonder of our particular lives, the sharpening of vowels from up north, the smoothing of –ings from down south, the inevitable unraveling at the point of a pen: a script of geography and kin and memory and desire.

The workshop meets twice a week, and it is the class itself, the communion of individual pursuit, that engages language and the personal life most profoundly. Imani and I, as team teachers in an unconventional environment, created an organic structure that responded to the needs of a class that changed daily. In the first weeks of the program, we had virtually no consistency in attendance. A woman with faux nails and fingerless gloves chain-smoking hand-rolled cigarettes was one of our first regulars. She had a natural dramatic flair that translated well into storytelling and writing. We would present the simplest exercise, and she, through her tales, catapulted us into foreign lands and herbal curatives, even a memorable proposition that the moon is indeed made of cheese.

Some days we had two students; other days, for no discernible reason, twelve. In direct conflict with the initial curriculum we had painstakingly devised—which was cumulative in nature—we learned to accommodate unpredictability by making each day sufficient unto itself and each workshop self-contained. We also had to plan activities that included women from all levels of literacy and a range of abilities: women functioning at more-or-less university levels of critical inquiry sat on the couch with students who could not read or write. This is no exaggeration. The scope of literary experience in the workshop continues to be a wild card; the optimism this forces out of structure is that anyone willing can create. This necessary standard sets a temper for the class, one of respect for expression and effort—and annoyance for intentional disruption. The entrance requirement for the class is willingness to write and respect for other writers; it's that simple.

We begin each workshop by honoring. In this ritual, a student states her name and gives thanks or honor to a person, place, concept, or emotion. We move from individual to individual: my name is Jeanie, and I'd like to honor family; my name is Imani, and I'd like to honor friendship; my name is Margaret, and I'd like to honor nature—until we return to the beginning of the circle of students and teachers. This formality has the effect of bringing us closer and acknowledging that all of us are equal in having elements other than ourselves for which to be thankful. It's an inclusive ritual: it has vaguely religious overtones, in part because many of the women honor their Higher Power (a term used in Alcoholics Anonymous), but its ultimate effect is something a little mysterious. I'm not clear, frankly, on why this simple ritual has such an impact, but it solders a unity of effort in workshop and bridges the gap between writing (with its active process of reflection) and the outside world more dependably than any other I've seen.

After honoring, Imani and I introduce the exercise of the day. We generally focus on one writer or theme, centering our brief discussion around it, examining an idea in several different ways, using poems, narratives, or even visual images. If the writing exercise concerns the importance of place, for instance, we'll read a poem or story that describes a place and discuss it at length or briefly, depending on the mood of the group. As the classes at the dinner program last one and a half hours, we have this luxury. From this central concept, we pose questions that we hope will serve as inspiration for the twenty to thirty minutes of writing that follow.

Nothing lifts the heart more than seeing these women bent over their notebooks, with no motivation other than the act itself, unselfconsciously following the thread of thoughts they themselves invent. There is head-scratching, murmuring out loud, sudden bolts for a cigarette, humming—what music! It is hard work to say what you mean. The limbs stiffen, the neck freezes, the entire body begs out of this unnatural effort while noises outside the thin walls beckon with gossip and snacks and coffee time. In this rapid technological age, writing seems downright stodgy. Thoughts seem plain as the nose on your face until you try to write them down. Notions are nearly audible, a thousand details clear, then paper, blank page, crumpled paper: why is it so hard? Writing is not an echo of last night's phone conversation. It does not merely replicate speech. It is a process of discovery and is, to a greater or lesser degree, always an effort of will.

Those students just learning to read and write illuminate perhaps most clearly how written language is a system and process of communication distinct from talking. Writing uncovers new memories and associations often held in check by the efficient mechanism of consciousness. That writing surprises the writer is the steadiest gamble. There is some radical operative reaching deep, through force of word and memory, which reveals novel associations so determinedly, in such humble drag, that students repeat almost daily: I'm not sure where this came from, or I haven't thought about this since I was a kid, or I started writing about blue vases and ended up talking about my grandmother.

For women who lagged behind in school in the past, the vaguely academic feel of our workshop seems to restore some faith in their intellectual abilities. To our surprise, some students in these unconventional environments embrace formality, taking notes, for example, and referring to the workshop as "school." I believe that participation builds a bridge to the intimate places and times we as instructors can never predict, but we try to support that bridge-building by including some typical trappings of a school setting. The writing workshop at the women's prison was designed in a semester model, concluding with a graduation ceremony and a certificate of achievement. The dinner program honors its writers by publishing a selection of their writing in an anthology and hosting a community Valentine's Day to celebrate the anthology with performance, music, and a reception.

Yet workshop exercises cannot turn back the clock or wave a magic wand over a life. Writing cannot make a woman clean and sober any more than I can quit smoking by watching you run a marathon. Neither can the most austere recovery programs "cure" a woman who cannot imagine that there is a viable and meaningful life for her in her community. Writing works the muscle of vision: it insists often on that which is not true, on fiction sometimes being more telling than fact, of invented texts that tell stories about people and places that suspend, even for moments, our thorough dependence on the outside world for truths about ourselves. Writing, finally, begs not only a concentration on the rich inner climate, but exercises an ability to envision things as they once were—or have never been but could be.

IN MY WORK with WritersCorps, I am a white woman working in a predominantly African-American environment. My supervisor is a black man, and most of my students at the dinner program and most of my fellow instructors are African-American. At the women's prison, Deb (my coauthor) and I worked as white women in a facility in which almost all of the inmates and officers were African-American. I have light hair and blue eyes and am 5 feet 9 inches tall. My heritage is a mixed bag of Norwegian, German, English, and the blurring that several generations on this continent can do. On the standardized forms that request racial identity, my box is White/Caucasian. Because of the racial history my students and I share, a huge crevasse splits open simply by virtue of our appearance. It's an awesome divide.

In the recently published anthology *Skin Deep: Black Women & White Women Write About Race* (1995), Marita Golden (coeditor with Susan Richards Shreve) ponders why so many black women like herself agreed to participate in this anthology, while white women, by and large, balked at the notion—usually, in fact, outright refused to participate. Golden, a well-known novelist, essayist, and teacher, confesses her own initial reluctance about the project. But she writes that this stage folded quickly to a real excitement:

> I was fiercely, totally excited by the prospect of working with a group of women prepared to step up to the plate on the one subject in America nobody really wants to discuss. Correction: whites don't want to discuss, and blacks can't *stop* discussing. Ironically, white America will catapult books about race to the top of the best-seller list, even as racism remains a national open wound. . . . And even bolstered by women's actual, yet often mythologized, talent for intimacy and revelation, race remains taboo even among the hippest, the most liberated, progressive, and righteous among us.

I have to admit to my own reluctance in raising the subject. But why are white women so unwilling to discuss race with black women?

In part, I believe, it's because there exists no strong historical precedent for such a dialogue. We have the 1960s as a model for groundbreaking, but from what I've read and heard, there was limited interracial sisterhood going on even in religious, antiwar, and civil rights grassroots organizations. Earlier still, some black women joined white women in the suffrage movement in the nineteenth and early twentieth centuries, but white women who lobbied eloquently for women's rights generally accepted that if and when women were granted the right to vote, black women would still be left out on the basis of their race. And while the feminist movement in this country is finally beginning to recognize that it also needs to examine the cultural foundations on which it continues to grow, it is far from a practical diversity. Women of color challenge white feminists to see that the same prejudices the movement professes to fight can be found in the movement itself—and not just toward women of color, but toward working-class women and lesbians.

At the dinner program, where my team teacher, Imani, is an African-American woman, we are able to provide an experience through our combined efforts that we never could have alone. There were black women who might never have come to class with me—who stared askance when I simply invited them—but who would attend the workshop based on their interest in Imani. In a society in which racial identity matters so much, it seemed clear to me that there was, for some, a barrier to participating in the workshop with me solely on the basis of race. In the same way, race was a deciding factor for white students considering the class: many would have been reluctant to attend had Imani been the only teacher.

At the women's correctional facility, the racial dynamic was exaggerated a hundredfold because Deb and I were two of the few white women there. The class suffered, from the beginning, from the limits racism imposes: although we had the endorsement of a black woman prominent in the community, we would always be alien to a central aspect of our students' identity. Individuals, I learned, can make the leap, but group dynamics, white or black, generally reinforce the racial divide still defined by suspicion, bitterness, even rage. Because of our physical appearances, Deb and I elicited some powerful stereotyping. Primarily because I have a mass of curly, waist-length hair, some assumed there must be more on my head than in it. Deb's voice is distinctly southern, so for some the first words out of her mouth invoked associations of slavery, Jim Crow, and the Confederate flag. We had to acknowledge these stereotypes in order to get beyond them.

Several months into the workshop, Imani joined Deb and me at the prison. One evening, we read out loud together several poems by contemporary black writer Michelle T. Clinton. That night, Deb was teaching elsewhere, so I was the only white person in the room. Subtly, underneath the visceral, unflinching imagery and dialogue of Clinton's poems, the racial climate in the room grew more distinct. Out loud, verse after verse, details of racial violence, the ramifications of a society formed and growing older deeply rent by institutionalized racism—the riots, sexual violence against black women and young black girls, white men black men white girls black girls, the denominator of skin color meaning so terribly much, smell of liquor after the eviction notice has been delivered, "slips" of tongue by white friends, details of a life not keeping quiet or nice anymore. Feelings swelled around the images as the black women in that prison classroom identified with calling out the racism they have experienced. Imani later said what made the difference that night was that the poems were naming names out loud. The central fact for me was that I was white and everybody else was black.

At one point in the discussion, one of the women crossed her arms and looked me straight in the eye. She had always been polite to me and probably believed that in some way I was different from other white folks because I did not display the racist behaviors she often encountered. But this night she lifted her finger, pointed at me, and said, "I want to know what YOU have to say about all this. How does it make you feel to hear all this about white people?"

In that moment, all the charged divisions flooded and hung around her words. In that moment, I was not a writer or a teacher or a woman; I was white. I tried to respond by drawing distinctions, nervously and nearly inarticulately, between individuals and cultures, but nobody in that room really cared what I had to say. The overriding emotion crackled around her question: that she said it to me in that environment, pointing her finger, and surrounded by painted cinderblock. The emotional pitch, already intense in the jail workshop, keyed up even higher the moment she spoke, and we crossed some invisible boundary. Because it is uncomfortable and because we yet live such separate lives, black women and white women rarely confront race *together*. Trying to do so that evening formed an experience I'll never forget and brought home to me the fact that, in my years with WritersCorps, I am as often learning as teaching.

As a white woman, I have participated in evading the hard words. Society has socialized white women to be "nice," and this politeness is anathema to the messy business of race dialogue. Uncomfortable issues threaten the nice girls because there is no sugar sweet enough to coat the potent thing that sets Los Angeles on fire or burns down small black churches across the South. I have frequently witnessed white women in feminist discussions on race burst into tears when the politeness scale tips. The race discussion railroads into hurt feelings and smoldering frustrations that ultimately end the discussion imperative to healing the racial divide. The conciliatory manner in which I myself have approached interracial conversations on race have concealed fear of what an honest assessment might produce. I'm not advocating disrespect and spleen-driven behavior. I am trying to detail the ways in which white women fail to connect; and that these failures doom us to repeat and refine the racial blueprint.

What we discovered in our workshops is that some folks do cross the racial divide—and that writing together helps. It's not that any of us stopped noticing our race; rather, we started noticing additional qualities in each other. The process of writing reveals the individual world, and because of this intrinsic value accorded the singular life, connections grew between women staring across the racial abyss. A creative community emerged against the odds that sometimes tentatively and sometimes boldly defied what could have been antagonistic boundaries. The relationships out of which this book emerged testify compellingly to the power of language to create a place for interracial dialogue that effectively empowers each speaker, regardless of race.

If, as I believe, we create healing and possibility from writing and literature, from what Terrence Des Pres calls the "vigor of our own interior music," then I have heard symphonies in the most unlikely of halls: in the inner city, or as poet Lucille Clifton—and I—like to call it, *home*.

TWO

CONNECTION AND COMMUNITY

Deborah Pugh

On the morning of September 12, 1994, when I turned on my television to catch the rush hour report, I expected to see a preview of the day's kickoff ceremony for President Clinton's AmeriCorps community service program. Instead, the stories were all about a plane that had crashed into the White House earlier that morning, killing the pilot but not hurting anyone else. Security personnel and aviation experts scratched their heads at the Cessna 150, its nose smashed from the collision right below the president's bedroom.

In the three years I had lived in Washington, D.C., I had never been on the White House tour. One time I had tried, but the lines were too long, and considering the grand house did not fit my definition of democracy anyway, I had not returned. This morning, however, clutching my engraved invitation to the AmeriCorps ceremony, I circled 1700 Pennsylvania Avenue and finally found the right gate to enter. It, of course, was the place where thousands of people were lined up. Other onlookers stood around the iron fence watching workmen remove the wreckage of the plane.

The crowd was the mixed bag one always sees in Washington. Many were AmeriCorps members themselves, mostly college students and recent graduates, their fresh faces shielded by black baseball caps. The expensive-suit crowd with their briefcases and tight hair were there too, shifting foot to foot in the snaking line. I must admit I was awed by the display of people and the clean magnolia grandeur of the White House; yet I felt uncertain, at the same time, about my ability to teach people the program application called "the underserved."

I had first discovered WritersCorps, the division of AmeriCorps devoted to writing programs, on the back of a publication put out by the Associated Writing Programs, a nonprofit organization of writers and creative writing programs. At the time, in April 1994, I was frantically finishing my masters thesis at George Mason University, teaching two sections of special topics in American literature as a graduate teaching assistant, and studying for my oral exam on thirty authors. I had also worked hard that year preparing an application for a Fulbright Award to go to Jamaica and write a book on Caribbean women writers. Although my proposal had been accepted in the first round of competition, it had not made the cut in the second round, so I was looking for a job that would make use of my teaching experience and allow me to do some service work at the same time. WritersCorps seemed the perfect fit.

President Clinton had first proposed a national domestic service program in May 1988 at the Democratic Leadership Council when he was a governor. As president, he had finally had the means to bring such a concept into being. I knew about the program's noble predecessors—John F. Kennedy's Peace Corps and Franklin Roosevelt's Works Progress Administration. I was especially thrilled with the idea that serving in WritersCorps would make me part of the same tradition as WPA writers who collected oral narratives from former slaves, playwrights and actors who produced plays that spoke to ordinary people, and artists who painted grand murals in public buildings.

At the AmeriCorps kickoff ceremony, tainted only by one smashed Cessna accordioned in the soil, some 850 new volunteers were clustered under the portico of the North Lawn, while more than 2,000 dignitaries stood on the lawn itself. All were taller than I, so the most I saw was the steel-gray top of the president's head.

And I never did locate the WritersCorps group. I found out later they had left the proceedings to meet at the Martin Luther King Memorial Library across town. Unfortunately, after waiting four hours, I had to leave to teach a class before the event began. I shuffled down the sidewalk past a Secret Service man with the unmistakable coiled wire disappearing into his collar. He was leaning on a table covered with AmeriCorps T-shirts.

"Hey," I said, "have you seen a group called WritersCorps? We're part of AmeriCorps." He was probably the fifth person I had asked.

"No," he said, looking tired of the whole affair.

"Can I have a T-shirt?"

He shrugged and told me to help myself.

As I pulled through the tangled pile, I heard some of the AmeriCorps oath booming out over the loudspeakers: "I will get things done for America to make our people safer, smarter, and healthier. Faced with apathy, I will take action. Faced with conflict, I will seek common ground. Faced with adversity, I will persevere. I will carry this commitment with me this year and beyond. I am an AmeriCorps member, and I am going to get things done."

Throughout my year with WritersCorps, I would recall these words many times as the realities of writing, government programs, and the streets collided with the program's ideals.

IN MAKING THE decision to apply for WritersCorps, I was not sure which part of me, the writer or the person, was signing up. By that time in my life, the two were so intricately entwined that the passion of one often ignited the other. I knew for sure that revolution begins first in the mind, and for me as a human being and a writer, I had arrived at the point of understanding that a space for freedom must be created inside before it can be accomplished outside.

When I began to work at the shelter and the jail, I knew what writing had done for me. It had brought me back from deadening silence; it had retrieved me from others' requirements that had shut me up and shut me down. In my life, my struggle had not come from my skin color. Rather, growing up poor among the privileged

and a lesbian among the straight created for me a feeling of straddling worlds to which I was bound but never a part. These worlds
constantly crashed together, leaving me with the options of either
pretending to be something I am not or fighting back and risking
the loss of opportunities, perhaps even life. It was not until I was
able to write that I became willing to recognize and face the fierce
and relentless agony of shame and self-hatred that I had internalized. Living in the margins myself allowed me to see the world with
different eyes; working with marginalized women enabled me to see
through theirs.

James Baldwin once said, "Know whence you came. If you know
whence you came, there is no limit to where you can go." This quote
is taped to the wall in front of me as I write to give me the courage
to be true to myself. It also constantly reminds me of the first time
I read it and realized I had to find my own language for my life. The
initial point of my discovery journey was my family, and emerging
from them put me on many paths—but it was a convergence of
those paths that brought me to WritersCorps. In many ways, I felt
as if I was on my way home.

From age one, when my parents divorced, until age eight, I lived
with my grandparents in Virginia. While my granny was a hard-
headed pragmatist, my grandfather, whom I called Pop, was a die-
hard romantic. That old man, my Pop, gave me some little spark,
for although he was uneducated, he knew how to love. He was also
the storyteller of our family and my spiritual guide. He would tell
stories about his father, who had died young, killed in a railroad
accident. He made his father, his mother, his childhood come alive
and, by doing so, helped me see how I was part of this heritage of
hard-working, proud people who helped each other and anyone else
in need.

I was my grandfather's shadow: everywhere he went, I went. My
Pop loved to walk the rails, a habit Granny would have had fits over,
but as he said, "What she doesn't know won't hurt her." It was as if
Pop and I were in a conspiracy, a world made of just him and me, a
world full of fun. When he and I were together, it felt as if he could

see through my eyes; he seemed thus to give me permission to see the world my way. When we walked, he'd tell stories about old hoboes who rode the rails and how he used to hop boxcars. We would be walking along, and he'd point to a house and say, "In that house lived some people; who were they?" Then it would be my turn to tell stories about the people. I don't remember those tales now, just bits and pieces, but the more imaginative I made them, the better, and we'd laugh and laugh. He'd pick me up, throw me on his back, and we'd walk some more. I still ride on that old man's shoulders.

It's strange how one incident can become life-defining. One day, my Pop and I were in the backyard splitting kindling for the coal stove. He stopped, pushed the sweat-stained fedora back over his forehead, and pulled me close. "People can take everything away from you," he said, "they can take your clothes, your food, but it's one thing they can't take. They can't take away what's in your head. You remember that, you hear?" In a way, I think the reason I remember his words so vividly is that it frightened me to think people could take away my clothes and food. Until then, I had lived in a world of faith and a feeling that what's important centered around having pride in yourself and loving other people. But at age eight, I discovered I needed my grandfather's words for guidance when I went to live with my mother and new stepfather—and found myself in a home filled with alcoholism, anger, fear, and violence. Suddenly, nothing made sense, and I fractured inside. It is a disruption I've spent years putting words to and healing from.

By the time I was fifteen, I was certain that if I did not go to college, I would die. Literally. The tension of violence had become so thick between my stepfather and me that I was sure one day it would all explode and only one of us would remain standing: I guessed it would not be me. But what my grandfather had told me that day splitting wood was still with me. I could not out-fight my stepfather, but I could out-think him. In college, I threw myself into novels and books of political theory, history, and sociology. In this world of middle-class privilege, people ate fried chicken with a knife and fork, and there were standards to be met on every front—don't talk loud, don't get drunk, don't raise hell, don't sing to the tiptop of your voice, don'tdon'tdon't. At home, of course, a contrary litany rang out—don't get above your raisin', don't get too big for your britches, don't act like you're better than everyone else.

Often I felt awkward, betraying myself with my obvious attempts at social graces. This was the pleasant, middle-class world I wanted, but there seemed to be entrance requirements I could not satisfy no matter how I tried. I would realize from things said or unsaid that "those people" everyone spoke of included me. Mexicans, African-Americans, gay people, and poor people: we were those who were labeled, stereotyped, dismissed with a word. But even though one day I flew into a tantrum when other students couldn't understand why Watts was burned during the riots, I never said how I understood. I was living a lie. Many lies.

One of the biggest lies was my sexuality. There was no vocabulary for it that I had encountered outside of Freud and the Bible. For the straight people around me, I knew that I was an unnatural abomination. Yet, since I had been like that for as long as I could remember, I could not understand why I was so bad. It had never been a choice; it was just the way it was. But I also knew what could happen if this fact were known, so I went further and further underground, not only in my daily activities but into myself. I hid huge parts of my life, particularly from my family. I could not jeopardize those people who loved and sheltered me, yet I had to alienate myself from them to protect my secrets. At times, when I wasn't repressing it, I felt Humpty Dumpty crash off the wall inside me. I would sweep up the pieces and place them neatly in a little bag that I kept deep in my silence. Not only was I distancing myself from others, but I was separating from myself. I had no words to embrace what was unacknowledged. And because there were no words, I could not embrace myself. I had become a stranger.

Then, in graduate school, someone brought an essay by Audre Lorde to a women's reading group I was in. I had not heard of Lorde before, but when I read that essay, my eyes were opened by

this one statement: "You cannot use the master's tools to dismantle his house." I had always thought that *was* the only way: get those
degrees, get that job, and then bring about change from that position. But Lorde's words touched the deepest part of me, breaking
years of illusion and changing me forever. The tools were mine, but
I had to find them. And then I had to find the courage to use them.

FOR ME, GOOD teaching has always been a revolutionary act, mod-
eled on the teachers in my life who invited, cajoled, and shoved me
to stretch where I never thought I could go. Yet in a university—
where I'd had my only teaching experience—you have a classroom
to which the same students come, sit down, and hopefully leave
with some worthwhile knowledge after the semester is over. My
methods of teaching had always been more learner-centered than in
the traditional lecture-oriented classroom, and I often invited chaos
into my class by standing on the desk crowing like a rooster and
summoning the students to follow my lead. But chaos became my
own powerful teacher when I made the transition from university
to community teaching. The tidy and potentially punitive structure
of the academic world has no corollary in homeless shelters and
prisons, where student participation is voluntary and grades are neither reward nor punishment.

Chaos reigned even in the world of language. People with little
experience in post-secondary education approach literature and
writing from a vast number of different levels, and I found that I
had to discover that level for each of my new students. Even the
word "writing" proved to have challenges. When I spoke of "writing class," my new students thought it referred to improving their
handwriting or perhaps letter-writing. Writing about one's own
life—my purpose for the class—seemed to many of them a dull and
fruitless endeavor. Self-expression, writing about my life, making up
poems—what was that all about? they wailed.

When WritersCorps began, some writers had already been teaching in the community, so their sites were established. The rest of us
were given the freedom to establish programs working with what-

ever "population" we chose. I knew that I wanted to work with women, helping them explore their voices, but I wasn't sure where to begin. Another WritersCorps member hooked me up with a woman preacher who had been doing spiritual workshops in the District of Columbia Correctional Treatment Facility for Women; the structure of that program was already in place, so we merely joined it. However, there was no such structure at Rachael's House, a drop-in shelter for homeless women in downtown Washington. My program there would have to start from scratch.

I arranged with the director of Rachael's to offer a two-hour class twice a week; then, before my first class, I visited several times to get the feel of daily events there. Rachael's House is a typical brick row house with ten-foot ceilings and ornate circular reliefs from which chandeliers hang. The walls, old plaster painted again and again over the years, are framed on top by ornamental frets carved in molding. With the exception of the circle of metal chairs with black vinyl seats in the living room, Rachael's House looks more like a home than a shelter. More important perhaps was the fact that, with the exception of delivery or maintenance men, no males were allowed there. I am not certain now if this was a house rule or a custom, but the result was that Rachael's was a place where women could let their hair down and be safe from what might lurk outside.

Most of the women who came to Rachael's stayed in other shelters at night. This is the system if you are homeless. You spend the night at one shelter, sleeping until reveille is blown. If there is time, you take a shower and prepare to leave. During the day, you must get something to eat, so if you don't have any money, you go to a day shelter like Rachael's to get lunch, look for a job, and attend programs until it's time to leave for a dinner program at the next shelter. After dinner, you return to the overnight shelter. All of this circuitous movement is very time-specific for, if you are late, you might miss the chance to eat or a place to sleep.

Like all homes, Rachael's had its rules. You could not come in if you were intoxicated or on drugs. You could not stay if you caused any fierce arguments or physically threatened someone. You could not sleep in the house. In exchange for lunch, you had to sign up for a program and a household chore, such as vacuuming the floor or helping prepare lunch. During the day, Rachael's hosted and facilitated a variety of programs. The most popular was the daily Alcoholics and Narcotics Anonymous meeting, but depending on her needs and interests, a woman could also attend discussion groups on women's issues, such as women and AIDS; job-hunting groups; individual counseling; computer training; Bible-reading classes; reading and literacy improvement classes; exercise classes; and my creativity/writing class. The house and its programs were open to any woman who did not have a home of her own. If she needed to shower, pick up some clothes, or get warm, Rachael's was open to her. As one woman there said about Rachael's, "This is the place you come to leave homelessness." The programs were designed not only to help women work through the absolute emotional crush of their condition, but to empower them to overcome the incredible barriers they faced by the sheer fact of being homeless.

The longer I worked at Rachael's, the more I realized there was a true community of women within those walls. Of course, there were occasional power struggles, arguments, and disrespect; not everyone finds her way to community. But for those who did, the very best values of humanity and womanhood permeated Rachael's and created the kind of world I had always wanted to be a part of. No matter what a particular woman was going through, the atmosphere provided hope and encouragement. Even the troublemakers were viewed as women in so much pain they were not ready to see what was there for them. And instead of being ostracized, they were allowed to live on the edge of the community and float there as long as they needed. The only requirement to enter the fold was that a woman had to be serious and authentic, not ego-driven: there is little room for pretension among people whose common denominator is homelessness. In fact, the idea that everyone is in the same boat is a great leveler of society's conventional categories by status and prestige. At Rachael's, the authority a woman had as an individual did not come from money in the bank, job or profession, family connection, or even skin color. The notion of authority was replaced by personal integrity and contribution of knowledge and experience.

The week before Christmas, I began my ten-woman discussion group with Audre Lorde's essay "The Transformation of Silence into Language and Action." I was a bit apprehensive about using this reading, thinking that Lorde's original audience was an academic forum but feeling it was important to me as a woman and a writing teacher to talk about how women are silenced. Well, not only did my new students catch every nuance of the essay, but the discussion afterward far exceeded my expectations.

At first, the women only scratched the surface of how they had been silenced in their lives. But eventually a sixtyish woman from Ireland who suffered from mental problems said she had been raped on the streets. This was the first time she had told anyone about it, but she worried constantly because she was terrified of contracting AIDS. This woman's courage in speaking created the safety zone others needed to begin to tell about rapes and other violence they had survived both before and since becoming homeless. Another woman said that she had discovered many years after the fact that her mother had prostituted her young son when she was at work. A woman in her early twenties said that her brother had molested her daughter. When she told us that her daughter was then in another state, she began to cry, and several of the other women moved closer to comfort her.

I remember sitting in my chair thinking two things: first, that these women had more character than did the lawmakers on nearby Capitol Hill, and second, that I wished Oprah Winfrey could see this. I wanted all of America to see what I can only describe as a spiritual epiphany. Observing so much courage, compassion, and unconditional love in that room, I suddenly realized that this is truly how the world should be—this is how people should treat each other. How ironic, I thought, that all of Washington was talking about political change, yet here in an old row house not twelve blocks from the Capitol, life found its voice and grieved for the times that voice had been taken away.

A FEW DAYS after that discussion, I taught my first writing class at Rachael's. I suspected I would have to lure the women to class, so I took my guitar, passed out lyrics to the five who gathered, and led the women in some sing-along songs, from bluesy numbers to civil rights songs. Then, after talking a bit about writing and creativity and how the techniques of writing lyrics compare with writing poetry, we began the exercise. I had tried to select work that would interest all the women, no matter what their educational level or their attitudes toward taking an English class. For this first exercise, I had typed up lines of poems by Etheridge Knight, Langston Hughes, and Gwendolyn Brooks and scored the paper between the lines so an entire line or individual words could be torn off. When I distributed the pages, I asked the women to use the lines and words to create their own poems. Two of the women composed their poems entirely from the lines I provided; the other three chose particular words and wrote their own poems. Afterwards, we read our poems out loud and discussed why we had selected the lines or words, what meaning they had for us, and why we had structured our poems the way we did. This nonthreatening, satisfying start went a long way toward promoting my class.

Vocalizing, in fact, became one of the class's most important facets. I knew for myself and from initial experiments that the women wrote better and with more confidence if we started with some breathing, voice, or performance work. Not only did these exercises seem to clear away old physical and emotional blocks, but they were a sneaky way to introduce as many women as possible to poets' words, techniques, and rhythms. The exercises also helped to open up women who spoke at a barely audible level or did not speak at all—often those who were newcomers to homelessness. Even those women who sat in the living room pretending not to listen could not ignore their courageous sisters who recited, sang, and sometimes even choreographed movements to poetry.

Although it may have appeared to an outsider that we were just jamming and having way too much fun, something else very important was happening. One day, a woman got up to read Maya Angelou's "Phenomenal Woman," an all-time favorite of the women.

She read it the first time with a timid voice, stumbling over the words, and sat down. Two other young women then picked it up, divided the stanzas, and flew into an amazing rendition, almost deifying the lines: "It's in the reach of my arms,/The span of my hips,/The stride of my step,/The curl of my lips./I'm a woman/Phenomenally./Phenomenal woman,/That's me." Not to be outdone, the first woman wanted to read the poem again. This time her voice smoothed out, catching the rhythms of Angelou's lines. I saw something click in her as if she was feeling her voice from a different place than in regular talking. It seemed she was hearing her voice for the first time, and it was that kind of hearing that is knowing.

As time went on at Rachael's, we moved from simple exposure to writing to deeper examination of writing forms and techniques. Interest had been established, and word was circulating about the writing class, but now the problem was location. In the beginning, classes had been held in the living room. That was good for business in that the maximum number of people could come and go, listen in for awhile, leave or participate. But now we were doing the type of writing that required an initial mini-lecture from me, discussion of exercises, and deep digging from the writers. The class had moved from merely talking about writing to the really difficult job of doing it. The constant ruckus in the public area disrupted our discussions as well as the women's concentration, so I asked the director if we could move the class to the computer room upstairs.

There I discovered what became a community of writers at Rachael's. We now had a room of our own. In our room was a table in the middle of the floor that allowed six writers to sit comfortably. Another table against the wall sat two. If there were more women, we would arrange chairs in a circle around the table. Each who came regularly had her own notebook and kept it with her from class to class. I locked up the others' notebooks in a closet for protection and for privacy after class. It was extremely important to these women that their words, experiences, and feelings were protected from prying eyes. Ensuring this protection created a bond of trust and respect among the writers and between them and me. Somehow when the door closed and class began, we separated from the world outside. We became special—simply by being our true selves, relieved of all the social masks.

This class had become a thinking space where, as one woman told a reporter doing a story on the shelter, "I just start thinking things I never thought I would and when I'm writing it, I think more, and things come out that I never expected." When that reporter asked about writing as therapy, another woman told her, "Well, if you mean by therapy that I can have my own thoughts and say my own words, then I reckon that's therapy."

The degree of trust needed for hearing one's own voice as well as sharing experiences did not come as quickly for some as for others. When one woman who was new to homelessness joined the group, I did not know at first if she was suffering from newcomer depression or was inherently withdrawn. For many classes, she simply sat and listened. Then, she decided she wanted to write, but she did not read her work aloud or let me read it. During that time, she would fill page after page and then rip them out of the notebook. Eventually, she began to let me read what she wrote, leave it in the notebook, and even share it with the class. As the weeks passed, this woman whom I had initially suspected might be mentally ill began to blossom into a writer with a warm, beautiful smile. One day, I remarked on the astounding change, and she responded in this way: "Before becoming homeless, I was always a loquacious and outgoing person. But people are so mean, I thought I'd better keep to myself and not let anyone know me. If people think you're crazy, they leave you alone."

If having one's own thoughts and saying one's own words were therapy, then writing never took on a more therapeutic role than at the end of class when everyone read what they had written. Not only were the women curious about each other's writing, but this reading out loud also provided the means for discussion. In this way, connections were made between individuals in a world defined by the loss of connections.

Two events marked important transitions for the writers at

Rachael's. From the beginning of the program, I had been typing the women's writings after class and giving them the typed versions. I felt that seeing their work in black and white made the program and their writing more real to them. The typed versions also provided them with a record of progress during the year. It was a little thing really, but it is amazing how it symbolized something lasting, something solid in a world where very little for them was enduring.

It had been the class's goal from the beginning to publish an anthology. When my computer disks were overflowing with the women's words, we began to organize the pieces and make editorial decisions about what to include. The day I distributed the reproduced and bound anthologies was a galvanizing moment. Women whom I had only seen hanging around and some I had never seen began asking for copies. The writers were pleased and flattered by the recognition, and the pride I felt for them and all their hard work was a true reward for me.

About the time the anthologies came out, the staff at Rachael's was organizing an open house for its board, contributors, and anyone else who wanted to come, and the director asked if our writers would do a reading of their works. Although they were nervous about speaking in public, they were willing to give it a try. For all of them, it would be their first reading. The open house was a study in contrasts—the visitors, mostly white and in suits and fine dresses, along with the homeless women who stayed to hear the reading and our writing group. But when it came our time to read, the writers commanded the attention of the crowd with grace, power of performance, and the written word.

IF WORKING AT Rachael's filled me with energy and hope, my experience at the D.C. Correctional Treatment Facility was a tumultuous roller coaster ride. It began with a December 1st launching of the program in which Jeanie (my coauthor) and I read from our work along with four other WritersCorps members. About twenty-five women dressed in dark blue, orange, or red prison jumpsuits shuffled into the activity room of sad cinderblock walls and plastic chairs. The top of our podium, held on by two thin threads of a wood screw, wobbled and finally fell off. When it had to be pushed aside, we felt naked in front of our audience, clutching our notes or the books from which we read. I read journal excerpts about watching a friend die of AIDS. This subject touched many in the chairs before us who were dealing with their own HIV status or that of family members. Jeanie read a piece on a rape, and Imani (Jeanie's team teacher) read one on incest.

But it was the reading of Maya Angelou's poem "Still I Rise" that set magic afloat in the room. At first, without invitation, a few of the women began mumbling "I rise" along with the reader. The chorus of jailed voices echoed and rose at each refrain, and by the end of the poem, all voices—the rough, the young, and the meek—spoke as one. I was not surprised at how this poem seemed to capture the collective experience of these women, but I was absolutely amazed that so many knew the poem.

This was the power of the word in action. It was what I believe every writer hopes for: one expression that sings with the hearts of many. I began to feel that what was coming out of this program was history in the making. If recorded nowhere else in any history book, it was an account, a screaming affirmation, of people who would otherwise go unnoticed in the story of this nation. And somewhere, even if only in torn pieces of copybook paper in a jail cell drawer, there would be the words.

That was how I felt in the beginning. But as time went on, a different battle began to rage, both around and within me. Part of the problem was the environment in which we taught. Many times I felt as if I were Joseph K. in Kafka's *The Trial,* searching among unanswerable quandaries, a nightmarish wandering without reason. Even as I stood outside on Monday nights waiting for the guard to buzz open the doors, I would have a choked-up feeling that would stay with me until I left. Often I wondered how a person could be incarcerated for months, not to mention years, and not be bone-mad on release.

Although friends would kid me about having a captive audience in jail, the exact opposite was true. Joining the program earned points for inmates in parole hearings because it was one of the few with educational objectives, but nowhere did the guidelines say that real participation was required. When Jeanie and I first met with the facility's program official and social worker, they had suggested that we construct a learning contract for our students, including penalties for unexcused absences, profanity, verbal and physical assault, and lack of participation. In retrospect, I wish that we had done that. However, both Jeanie and I, in our early optimism, wanted to believe that behavioral controls were not necessary if what we offered was real. Our ideals and our patience were put quickly to the test.

We had not anticipated—nor known enough even to think of anticipating—the impact on our students of being locked up day after day after day. Every moment of every day is planned and administered by an authority over which the inmates have no influence or redress. There are rules that must be followed; however, the routes to power, influence, and authority differ. Egotism and deception would prevent one's being accepted in the community at Rachael's, but they seemed the only way to gain power in jail. The environment into which we entered reflected a pressurized and dangerous combination of anger, frustration, and helplessness.

In our first class, the Reverend Norma Jennings led a guided meditation. Her theory was that an individual's emotional and spiritual blocks must be cleared before any other life-work could be done. We agreed, recognizing that writing was an excellent way to encourage and develop problem-solving, critical thinking, and awareness. After the meditation, Jeanie and I spoke about families and storytelling and the importance of both to our sense of ourselves. Then, we gave the women an exercise to write a story handed down within each's family. Although they were enthusiastic, few could recall any family stories. One woman finally wrote about a cat and dog she had as a child; another wrote about a little girl who did not have brothers or sisters and had lived a lonely existence with her grandfather until she turned to bad influences on the street. When I approached a young woman who was having difficulty getting started, she spit out at me that her mother had never told her any "damn stories," so she wrote about the time her "homey" was gunned down and she stepped over him to get home.

In the first classes, Jeanie and I focused on definitions of writing, along with goals and objectives for the group. Although the women in jail were generally more widely read and politically aware than the homeless women at Rachael's, some seemed unable to move from talking about ideas and experiences to writing about them. And for those who wanted to write, the clash between them and the talkers created significant tension. As a facilitator, I found this competition to be a nightmare. From the outset, Jeanie and I had tried to create a physical and mental space in which democracy ruled — a learning environment in which there was no authority except the written word. We wanted to meet the needs and expectations of all of our students, but still to go about the business of writing — which in the end cannot be defined in any way other than closing one's mouth and putting words on paper. Not that we as teachers were exclusively outcome-oriented, but it became increasingly frustrating to us as well as many students that the most vocal members of the class were constantly derailing discussions of writing and actual writing time to vent their own agendas, challenge the teachers, or get attention.

Another issue we had to face and respond to was race. With a few exceptions, all of the inmates were African-American, as were almost all the staff. Jeanie and I, lily-white, came into a black world and had to deal with prejudices about our skin color. I'm not sure if anyone questioned our motives: I don't think they thought we were hated "do-gooders" or that we were making big money teaching there. But for some women, race was a river, and it took a long time to build even the flimsiest bridge. I was somewhat prepared for this sort of distance because of my experiences at the shelter. One day, for instance, an African-American student who had been looking at a picture of a lynching called me over. She pointed to one of the lynchers in the picture and asked if that was my uncle. When I said sarcastically that I didn't see any family resemblance, she said, "Surely you being a southern girl, your family owned slaves." I could only respond that to my knowledge, they had not. But this history and the awareness of pervasive, continuing racism in our society seemed always below the fragile surface. One night at the jail, the women presented a show they had organized for themselves, and because many of our students were in it, one of my co-teachers and I attended. It was a great thing really—so much talent and creativity. Then, for one of the skits, several women donned white hoods and dragged another woman to a noose hanging from the basketball hoop. After the mock lynching, another inmate sang Billie Holiday's "Strange Fruit." As the only white person out of a hundred or so women, I did not feel frightened or guilty; mostly I felt invisible. But a wash of sadness overcame me as I realized how forcefully the meaning of this skit was festering in these women's hearts. Always, as James Baldwin said, history is upon our brows.

Time did eventually allow us to make connections with at least the regular participants in the jail program. At the last class, our most rebellious student announced, to my astonishment, "This class has taught me many things and it's special. . . . All of us are special, and I've come to respect and love people who I never thought I could." Then, she looked at me. Whether she and I had crossed one bridge of race or she had just decided to stop locking horns with me, I don't know; but for all the ups and downs, I felt we had made some progress.

For most of the inmates, writing remained a first draft explosion of feelings and experiences; writing as a process from exploration to final draft required more commitment than some could give. But for those women who were writers or wanted to be, we were able to work with them individually to fulfill their objectives for the class. And another woman, who could neither read nor write when she entered jail, made remarkable progress. She had been participating in a literacy program, so our class supplemented her unwavering efforts to enter the world of books. Working with her through illiteracy and dyslexia to find the words to express her unforgettable voice gave me the courage many times to continue.

MY EXPERIENCE WITH the women in the WritersCorps programs certainly reinforced a powerful lesson: focus on the positive and what you can do, and leave what you cannot change behind. Many times I would scream into my computer from the frustrations of dealing with government bureaucracy. One of our fundamental problems was that WritersCorps and what it hoped to achieve could not be validated by number-crunching. As writers and teachers, we could not provide AmeriCorps or Congress with the statistics of success they seemed so urgently to require.

Many times I longed for the opportunity to sit down with an AmeriCorps administrator to talk about WritersCorps. But during my entire year, I was visited only once at my site, and the Ameri-Corps representative observed my class for approximately forty minutes. She furiously scribbled notes, but only spoke with the participants in the most superficial way. I wondered what she could possibly have gained in understanding from this brief encounter: How could she have seen from that short time how difficult it was to get people to trust, to convince women to break years of emotional isolation and allow themselves to open up, and to see how writing develops analytical, problem-solving, and employment skills?

In spite of our frustrations, WritersCorps members fulfilled President Clinton's oath. Jeanie and I set out to open a space in which writing and literature had validity, purpose, and usefulness. What we found was that some of the women had been experimenting in the arts long before our arrival, so our class provided for them a haven where their urge to create was respected. For these women, our classes became communities of literary endeavor in which all of our curiosities and observations beat together, leading to wild, excited learning and writing.

For those women who had not previously given voice or action to their creativity, our classes were an entirely new experience—an environment of acceptance and nurturing that was theirs simply by attendance. There were no criteria for admission: no confessions to be made; no concessions to be given; no entrance fees to be paid. We had only two rules: respect your voice, and respect the voices of others.

In this way, Jeanie and I carved out a space for a creative community of women writers. In the process, what we discovered went beyond writing, as we witnessed the empowerment that comes from simply loving people and accepting them for what and where they are. Creating and perpetuating this community required tremendous courage and commitment from all the women involved; yet all of us succeeded, each in her own way. This success shows that new paradigms of community can be built and sustained. The women's work in this book serves as testament to that.

Five Women Learning, Writing, Teaching

THREE

"LET IT BE AN EXPERIENCING JOURNEY"

Gayle

I have chosen to tell my story because of the memories that have always been so ever-present in my mind.

Over and over, I have written down my painful experiences to help me understand what has happened to me over these years. What I have come to understand is that I am blessed. Blessed to know that God has given me this life and these experiences to share with others so that they might come forth. Blessed, in this way, to give others strength and to live again myself. Even though my pain was overcome, I never suffered, not once, because I feel that my faith I grew up with was stronger than anything I could ever imagine. My faith gave me life today, and I have a life knowing that with God first anything can be possible. I would like to help others by letting them know that, if they are still alive today and have been through pain, they are blessed. Because they have a mission in life to find happiness and peace. To find a God of their understanding and go out and enjoy their life and to take one day at a time because can't nothing change what has happened in the past. The present can be so fulfilling as it has been for me.

Also, I have written my story for my children so that they may understand why I let my family raise them. So that they wouldn't be lonely growing up. So that they can see what kind of life I had and to make their lives better.

IN THE BEGINNING, my life was so simple. I was a child growing up with aunts in a household worshipping the Lord. My grandfather was a preacher, and my grandmother was a dear and compassionate woman. We always had love, sharing, and fun. We always had the best of times.

I was born out of wedlock on a lovely summer evening. My grandmother came to the hospital and took one look at me and named me, and I remember that it was good.

I lived in a house on a hill. Across the street was a graveyard and a big factory sitting at the bottom. My grandmother's house was about one mile from the store. It was like living in the country even though it was in the city because it was a small town and everyone knew everybody. The inside of the house consisted of this long hallway and a bedroom on the right side which was my grandparents' room, a bed in the hallway against the wall for grandkids, a bedroom on the right in the back of the house, a huge kitchen across from it, and a big back porch which held the bathroom. Our house had a full basement under the whole house in which my grandfather stored our wood, coal, odds and ends on one half. He had a tool shed in the other half because he was a carpenter, a jack of all trades. He could fix anything and build anything. A grapevine sat in the back yard, along with an apple tree and a row of chicken coops. Our dogs were also chained to that side of the house. On the other side was a long sidewalk from the back to the front. I can best describe our house as a castle because, even though it was small, it was fit for a king. My grandfather even built on another room because we were a big family.

I remember coming home and everyone loved me. I especially remember getting my first tricycle from my uncle. I was around five years old and it was a pretty red model for my birthday, and oh, I was so happy. I would ride and ride around in circles and up and down the street every day for hours showing other kids what I had because everyone had kids in my neighborhood too. But my family was the biggest.

My life as a child was active, always alive, always doing something whether it was games, friends, boys, or duties. Though my mother drank and we lived a life of violence, partying, and abuse, we lived traditionally with values and principles and understood that this was our life and we had to live it. We were chosen, and we had to make the best of it. We grew up as a family fighting for each other and just having a normal, basic childhood.

Nevertheless, I grew up an angry, resentful, lonely, and hurt child because I couldn't show emotion. I never said to my mother that I loved her. I never showed her I really cared what she said mattered because I was taught to be in control, show no mercy, and don't be a baby. No compassion whatsoever. I only was taught to be shut in my own self and deal with my own problems by myself. So I became an isolated, self-destructive person, always putting myself in destructive situations. Hoping against all hope that I would live through it because of watching my mother's life. So much violence and abuse in the name of love. I just didn't understand it then, but I understand it all now.

My sisters were the greatest. It is four of us and I'm the oldest. I gave the orders and they followed suit. It didn't matter what went down the wire, they were my backup. Except when it came to getting punished. They got most of the whipping. We played together out in the yard, and everywhere I went they went too. We would sit and talk about how we felt and what we wanted to do when we grew up. And to tell you the truth, we didn't turn out so bad. As a matter of fact, my next to the oldest sister has a nice family, stable security, and a job she's been working at least for twenty years. A very, very good husband, and three lovely children. They own property and are doing well. But my sister has one flaw which is built-up anger, and she doesn't mind expressing it. Because of the history. She always was my best friend and the only person I would listen to and would calm me down. She was always there for me when I needed her for anything or any problem. She is raising my two sons. I learn to be thankful today for her.

My next sister is very special to me. She is next to the baby, but she looks like me, so they say. We used to go places and everyone would say that we look just alike. I thought their imagination was working overtime because we don't resemble at all. We do share some form of bond. When I lived out of town, she would come and visit me on my birthday every year. We would fuss, and I would send her home. But one particular time she came and she stayed. I was always a big sister to all my sisters and they looked up to me, but I loved that sister most of all because she was truly following behind me. My baby sister was a spoiled brat, always crying and always getting us in trouble. But we would hold her, love her, and take her with us everywhere we would go. Also, I have one brother, and he was a little monster. He was always getting a whipping. I thought he was the stubbornest person in this world, and I was the one to beat the sense into him. But we played together, and we went and did things together because I was the oldest and I had to watch over them. We played, and when I got mad, we fought. I always won though.

We had a lot of relatives. A host of cousins and nephews. Although we had our differences, we were a family. We celebrated our grandparents' fiftieth anniversary one summer afternoon, and my whole family attended. We had a cookout and a family gathering that was memorable because we all got along that day and had a good time.

I remember my grandmother saying one day that, after having spent nine years with her, I had to go and live with my mother instead. My mother and father came and took me away that day and I remember I was crying and so sad. We went and picked up my other brother and sister and were strangers to each other, for they had lived in foster care. We lived in a house that had an upstairs and a downstairs. My sister and I had a room on the right at the top of the stairs, and my brother's room was on the left. My parents' room was downstairs, and in the back were the kitchen and bathroom. The living room was at the front of the house, and we were joined together by another apartment next door where another family lived. At first, there was a lot of fussing and fighting going on, but it turned out okay. We enrolled in a school at the top of the hill. I remember fighting every day because I was an angry and mean child when I was growing up. There was no one to beat me but my mother and father.

This was my first real understanding in seeing alcohol abuse in the household. Seeing the nature of violence and violence acted out. My first true learning of a family torn apart by words, drinking, and violence, and feeling pain and hurt. The first funeral of my best friend, of feeling the sadness, but never crying to my pain.

I remember my father was on the road a lot for his job, and he would leave us for weeks. My mother would party, and when he got home there would be these awful fights and my father got kicked out of the house. He finally couldn't take it anymore and left for good.

After that, my mother went on what I know now as a drunk. Always drinking, always drunk, always getting violent. Either she was fighting or she was going out on a stretcher every weekend. I felt so ashamed that I started running away from home. I was twelve years old, but thank God I had somewhere to go. For I ran to Grandma's house and she would be sitting on the front porch and I would sit down and talk to her and she would say that I was in God's hands now and I was going to be all right and for me to go back home because she couldn't keep me anymore. So I would go back home.

And I would act out by fighting or stealing until my father had to come back in my life. He came and took us for the summer to live with him in Washington, D.C. I went to visit my dad every summer in Washington after the separation. I was always a quiet child. I portrayed what people wanted to see from me.

WHEN I WAS fifteen, I lived with my mother for the summer because my father didn't pick us up for vacation. I started drinking because my mom drank as long as I can remember. I always had a lot of boys around me. Chasing me, running around and getting drunk. On one particular night, my boyfriend's friend got me drunk and raped me and I got pregnant with my son. I remember feeling hurt and love at the same time without really any understanding of what had happened because no one prepared me for this. There was no education of date rape at the time.

I turned sixteen years old when I gave birth to my son. After giving birth, I got strung out on sex. I dropped out of school and became what I felt was a loser to life. I felt my mother hated me and I hated what she was—a drunken woman whom I had to help home and then watch go through one beating after another by men who she said loved her.

When I started drinking, I felt good at what I thought was making love and I became caught in a world that some of us can understand. The assumption that I was in love became totally a false realization of who I wanted to become and what sex meant to me. For me, drinking seemed to ease the pain of making love and I felt like that was the thing for me. I would be in this relationship and we would be in love, but every time we made love, we would be drunk. It made me feel whole. But something was so very wrong, and I didn't know what it was at that time. I had used a lot of men in my life. Telling them what I wanted in a relationship, then giving something different. The sex part of a relationship is painful because of what I have experienced. And now, after having sex in a relationship, it falls apart because I cannot accept what sex has to offer and that is pain.

When I was seventeen years old, I met this guy who moved me into his home and stayed drunk too. I went back to school. I never knew he was abusive until he made me so mad, I snapped and said some of the meanest things until he went off. He cheated on me, he lied to me, and he stayed drunk. But I stayed with him, giving him my second child, a daughter. I was eighteen years old. After that I had gotten tired of his ways and tried to leave him. I left him a total of five times, and on the fifth time I succeeded but not without violence.

The violence began when I left the second time because I found him with another woman. But he stalked me; he manipulated me by using our daughter to see me. I loved him so much. He would wait at my mom's house until I got home and would try to beat me, but my mom intervened.

But one night, she couldn't help me. He had gotten drunk. I had borrowed his car, and he thought I was out on the street partying. But I wasn't. He wanted sex. I said no. He slapped me and I slapped him back, and as I turned to run, he pulled out his gun and shot me in the back. As I fell to the ground, I said, God forgive him for he knows not what he's done. And my life flashed before my eyes of always getting a whipping from the age of five years to now. Always getting punished for being a bad girl, for something I had done wrong. But I hadn't done anything wrong to die for that night. So I got up and sat on the step and told him, I forgive you. But I will never forget what he had done.

I forgave him enough to go back to him and as far as to go and pick out rings to get married. But as I looked at my finger and looked at him, I said, no way was I going to be in misery the rest of my life. The suffering never stopped, not by a long shot.

I was nineteen years old. My life took on a scared and timid form of men and sex and love. I lost all feelings for men in relationships as far as love was concerned until I became pregnant again at the age of twenty. I thought I had everything planned not to have any more children, but I did, and my son was a very special someone in my life. But a pattern formed where I started going back and forth to jail to escape the miserable life I was living. I was a twenty-one-year-old woman living so lonely until I just wanted to die. I tried to commit suicide at the age of twenty-two, but Jesus pulled me through yet another time. I have always had this misconception that I could find one man to marry and live the rest of my life with.

After I turned twenty-three, I realized that my life was meaningless and that I would never settle down because of what the man who shot me put me through. I went through men like money, never being satisfied because I didn't want the abusive life I felt they had to offer. That was until I went to prison for nine months and learned what it was like to be by myself. Then, it didn't feel necessary to have men in my life anymore. But then, I met my husband.

I met my husband after I had gotten out of prison. He had been released a few months before me. He stood right by my side faithfully for a year and a half. It was a relationship in which we had togetherness and love, which strengthened me to trust and be strong. He was five years my junior, but I felt he really loved me for me. And I learned to love him unconditionally. Even though I knew it wasn't going to last forever because of my fears, the relationship grew into something special. We would sit down and talk about anything under the sun. I had finally found someone who had patience, love, and understanding.

But he also had faults I had no compassion for. No sympathy was I willing to give this man. Not even an ounce of recognition. So he started screwing around, and so was I. Until we talked about it. We could talk about anything and come upon an agreement that if we got caught, we would suffer the consequences because of our actions.

We got married. Our marriage was a competitive marriage: me trying to stay busy, and him trying to keep secrets. He ended up getting caught and lost me the day after I threw him out. But the love never died, and I had a friendship that even I couldn't understand. He had become a part of me. I loved him so very much. Till death do us part, I said. I stuck by this man until he said it was the end. I feel I got blessed for this particular relationship and that it gave me some freedom.

AFTER MY HUSBAND and I separated, I started smoking crack cocaine. I really got started doing drugs at the age of seventeen. After having my first child, my aunt said it was ok to take my first joint. I smoked reefer till I was twenty-seven years old. The feeling it gave me was eerie and light-headed. Before I started smoking, I prayed that the Lord would watch over me and let it be an experiencing journey, and not let me get too far gone that I couldn't find my way back. So the journey begins with life on cocaine.

My journey into drugs was self-centered tripping because I used it as an excuse and defense to keep my husband away and a selfish excuse for doing what I had seen my friends do. I thought I was having a good time looking forward to smoking crack. There are a lot of stories I could tell about the world of drugs. But I just want to remember the hold that my conscience had on me. It wouldn't let me go all out. Of course, everyone does what they have to do to get high; but for me, that meant watching people come and go in my life, my kids, my family and so-called friends. Watching people go through prostitution, blow jobs, beating, drug dealing, and stealing and selling things (TVs, food stamps, etc.). Watching people not thinking about themselves as they fell deeper and deeper into the pit of hell. Never realizing they were abusing themselves, their bodies, and their minds, until it put them where they were safe from themselves—jail, detox, hospitals, death. They just wouldn't understand. We were losing our minds and felt it for sure, but just couldn't do anything about it then. I did: I prayed!

My drug of choice is crack cocaine, and what it does for me is relaxes my body tensions and lets my mind into its own world. When I smoke, I feel the drug working the minute I take the first hit. I start to feel relaxed. Being high means being consumed by the drugs I smoke until I'm tired. Getting high is relaxing to me because from the first hit, I found it to be that way. I am a very depressed person and nervous of life most of the time, so I choose to smoke.

I call crack my friend because I understand why I smoke. I know what it does for me. It takes the place of people, places, and sometimes sex. I prefer to smoke crack because of the lifestyle I lead. No promises, no dreams, and I don't look forward to a future.

I never got high by myself. I always had a friend who turned into my enabler. I always gave them the most so I could watch them get high. Watch how they would inhale that smoke, how long it would take to blow it out and their reactions afterwards. Always giving myself a choice of whether I wanted to act like they did. And most of the time, I would find myself acting like that anyway because it had become such a pattern. When I had spent my last dollar smoking, I met this big time drug dealer who wanted to use my place. But I wanted to use him, and we turned into good friends after he had seen the way I stood for something (I didn't know what at the time). I guess all the people I smoked with and copped from saw that, because they put space in between visits to see me. So to make up that time in between, I shoplifted to support a $500-a-day habit. I never felt I had a habit. I just wanted to smoke because I promised my husband I would be smoking until he came back to me. So I began a partying trend, looking forward to smoking every day.

I chose to keep stealing until I got busted. I went to jail three times over two years for three to four months each time. Each time, I got closer to the God of my understanding. He pulled me through to experience some more suffering through smoking some more. Because I had a choice: I wanted to smoke cocaine in my life to replace that feeling of hurt and disappointment that had ever come into my life, the man I gave up, and my loneliness. I was so self-conscious that I locked me away and became this cold, careless person. No one could hurt me but myself. That's the way I became.

I lived in a city with no family, and I had a circle of select friends that enabled me to get high just by hanging out, no sex, no force, no play, just watching them do what they had to do to get us high. Sometimes I became guilty and wanted to try it, but when I did, bad things happened. I know only the grace of God pulled me through.

Like the time I went out with a girlfriend prostituting and got picked up on my first date ever. He was a nice guy and everything, but in the end, he pulled out this 357. Didn't do nothing but get high and got fucked.

So I knew that prostituting didn't apply for me, but that didn't stop me from trying it a couple more times and succeeding. For I remembered I had a husband and my conscience was stronger than anything I had ever done. So I fell back on my enablers, waiting on them to get me high. But I had to accept and realize it wasn't ours, wasn't my coke we were smoking. It was my girlfriend's, and she worked hard for it. I had to take what I got until I found my own and my own way. My own way was finding a man that got high. I knew I wasn't going to work from the start, but he was in an accident and was going to come into some money. I let him move in with me. Little did I know he was a hustler, and that was when the trouble started. After a few months, I hit many bottoms during my drug use, but the one I remember most was waking up one morning and discovering I couldn't move. I had come to the end of the road. But God pulled me through again. Praying, learning the word, and sleeping with my Bible by my side, I had found relief.

The effect drugs had on my body had taken a drastic play. It had absorbed all my body fluid, and I lost weight, a whole thirty-five pounds. I was a walking skeleton. I couldn't move at all sometimes for days. I kept praying, asking for forgiveness for letting myself fall prey to this experience. I had prayed for and I had hoped to find strength to recover from this kind of suffering. I was in shock at what I had allowed to happen to me. It took about a week of just being sick, and all this time this man kept operating without me. People were in and out of my apartment all the time.

After getting my strength back, I came to the conclusion that I didn't need him. I could kill myself by my own hands. After he had smoked every dime, he had to go. He just had to. He left, but his customers still came and spent money and smoked. He got so jealous and paid a smoker to beat me up. I ended up with a big lip and a gash in my head, but he was in worse shape than I was. Again, God had other plans because He gave me the strength when I needed it to do something important.

I have always talked to the Lord, and I cling to my Bible asking the Lord to let my experience come to an end because I felt I had learned and lost enough. I learned that smoking crack is deadly: it's a very real experience with the world in cruelty and violence. With sick emotional weaknesses and perverseness from others, I learned that a person with no will or willingness for life smokes crack. I learned that your mind reaches a very depressing state when you take that first hit and try to think. And you know that smoking crack does not make your life better, but you want to smoke anyway. Because all you see and all your friends do is smoke crack and you are lonely and want to be part of the crowd.

I have lost my life for five years. I have lost my dreams and goals.

I have put my life of happiness on hold because I wanted to experience a life of suffering by smoking crack. A life of not wanting to work, not wanting to raise my children around drugs, not wanting to enjoy day-to-day living or responsibility because I'd rather be getting high with people. That was all I seemed to have in my life. And thinking about them, things seem like yesterday, but it has been five months. And I want to live today, and I will because the Lord has given me His blessing to live another way. I have found a peaceful joy I never felt before, and by God, I aim to keep it.

What brought me into the Alcoholics Anonymous (AA) and Narcotics Anonymous (NA) program was a guy I met at work. He offered me a room in his apartment, and I took it. I knew that, after I moved in, there was a hidden agenda, but I stayed there anyway. He introduced me to an AA meeting, and I started attending every day. I felt good, and I met a man. But one particular night, my friend was coming by the apartment. So my roommate decided to take a dealer's package from someone dealing in front of where we lived. When he ran back inside, the dealer and some of his friends kicked down the door and beat him out of the apartment. They chased him down the street, but he got away and I was grateful. But they came back to the apartment and started harassing my friend and me, asking us where their stuff was. I told them we didn't know, but they kept on and on about their stuff, saying we had it. They robbed my friend and pulled out a knife on us. I feared for his life as I watched them hit him and intimidate him. The guilt of being helpless really brought me to shame because he was innocent and I wasn't: my roommate and I had gotten high before he came and had smoked up the dealer's stuff. From the information I had accumulated, I now knew the next time I started to smoke would be even worse. Getting into a situation and not knowing whether we would come out of it alive changed me. I had never experienced something like this before. Before this time, someone else was always getting in trouble and I would be on the outside. But this time was different. I was in the middle and brought someone else with me.

IT TOOK ME five years to get to the point in my life where I felt my prayers were being answered and that I might go into recovery. How I finally arrived at this point was, first, I got drunk and went into detox. After I got there, I prayed to God that I would see it through. I became willing to take any suggestion anyone had to offer. I came to realize that my life was full of depression and it stemmed from within. I made myself suffer for so long, but tried to keep my mind open to the possibility that there was some good in the things I could do. I see what others go through with drugs in their lives, and I asked myself, do I want to go through it? What will I accomplish from it? Is it going to make my life better?

I will be an addict for the rest of my life. I sometimes wonder what I will be addicted to next. Hopefully, the Lord Jesus Christ. I have been praying that he will guide me to be happy, prosperous, and to help others like myself. I feel good in knowing that I took this step to change my life and that I'm doing what I have to do to get this thing called recovery.

Now trying to recover from the pain I allowed myself to go through, I have come to realize that no one will give me a chance unless I give myself a 100 percent of me. The way I talk and the feelings I share will need to change. The outlook was grim, but I am willing to go to any length to stay clean. I have to learn that I will change in spite of myself if I stay with the twelve-step program of recovery. I try so hard to be patient and accept what I cannot change. I work hard at being peaceful and happy on the inside as well as on the outside. Sometimes, I still get caught up in my own emotions because I know what the outcome will be. But to know the Lord is to know wisdom, and to have knowledge isn't always easy. Being shot and having my life flash before my eyes is something only my God and I can understand. I'm being very careful of my life one day at a time, because I have to account for the pain I cause others. I must stop inflicting pain on myself that way. Growing up has some good points and some bad points, but I must remember where I am today and try to think about the good things only. Where I am today is a person trying to grow up and make a way to live productively on my own or in a relationship under the guidance of God. The choices I make will be prayed on first and foremost.

The most important thing about me today is change, along with my willingness to be patient and happy throughout the day. Thanks be to God always for giving me this opportunity to live in faith and believe that He does supply our needs if I remain true and honest to myself.

Even though the past was painful, the future is going to be very bright if I just hold still and allow Him to do His will. I had to first admit I had become powerless over my alcoholism and addiction and that my life had become unmanageable. And now I keep my life that simple and live one minute at a time under the guidance of the God of my understanding.

DISCUSSION

Jeanie Tietjen

One early winter evening last year, I looked past the frozen reach of tree limbs into a sky full of stars. In myth and travel, we have used the constellations to guide us, invented gods around their luster. On this night, I was walking from the train station, reflecting on the dinner I'd just had with Gayle, hearing her voice in my mind, and I thought: addiction is her lodestar. Addiction is that navigational point around which the rest of her adult life clusters and rotates. Its false and powerful radiance has been her primary source of pain; but now, in her recovery, it is the beginning of sobriety, the compass that guides her story, and the dilemma she must reconcile to find the healing she desires.

When I first met Gayle at the Dinner Program for Homeless Women at the First Congregational Church in Washington, she was working as assistant to Linda, the program director. This job of helping set up the dining room, making sure the women sign their names before taking a seat, and leading the Narcotics Anonymous/Alcoholics Anonymous (NA/AA) discussion group is esteemed among the women because it signifies Linda's trust. Being assigned this responsibility makes the woman who holds the position different, suggests a bridge between homelessness and a life with a job and a home. Gayle knew almost all the women by face if not by name and greeted them happily at the door. She sat on a chair by the entrance, smoking and chatting and keeping an eye on things, calling out to the women "hello" and "coming to group?"

In our writing class, Gayle was the bright and extroverted student. She seemed to want to talk about everything, to connect, to express. She thanked her Higher Power every class for letting her wake up that morning. Her vitality moved her around the room, in her seat, out of her seat, talking constantly with one or more of the other writers. Her hair was curled one day, laid back neatly in pins the next. She painted her nails and kidded me about my casual dress, all the time with an unbelievable light coming from her face. She chafed at the regulations of the transitional house where she lived then, but abided rules like the curfew as insurance against what she called "running around." Homelessness seemed incongruous with this exuberance. Gayle was on her way out of homelessness, I felt sure. Her energy and dedication to a clean, sober life proclaimed this ambition every day.

After a few months at the dinner program, my team teacher and I began to enjoy regular attendance from five or six women in our class, including Gayle. We studied Maya Angelou's *I Know Why the Caged Bird Sings* and other women's memoirs and autobiographies, and we discussed the influence of autobiographical form in fiction. Inspired by these writings, we focused our workshop efforts around telling stories of our own lives. Exercises explored personal history through images (describe your neighborhood), home cooking (what is your favorite dish and tell one story about it), and character (describe your mother). Writing about events such as their first kiss and their most memorable birthday encouraged the women to capture their lives for all of us to hear. This communal, active witness to those elements that shape a life was often joyful because it connected us, bringing the private into the collective where a memory was a gift to share. It created an environment of trust and respect that, though limited, had an impact deep in the private world of each writer.

From the first, Gayle's voice stood out. Before I asked her to contribute to this book, she was already writing testimonies. In name and form, testimonies emerge from the language of drug and alcohol recovery groups. Telling your whole life story is part of the process of overcoming addiction; it is a way of facing the consequences of addictive behavior on your life and on those closest to you. By telling the whole truth, or as nearly as you are able, especially in the presence of others in recovery, you shed the deceptions that have kept you in a painful dependency. Sober, the speaker of a testimony can make a distinct break from the addictive past.

In the introduction to her memoir, Gayle explains that she "has chosen to tell my story because of the memories that have always been so ever-present in my mind." The story she has chosen to tell is not the only story of her life, but it is necessary to her future. The immediacy of her voice, as if her words spill directly from her mind's eye onto the page, delivers memory breathlessly, urgently. Her text is vivid because her struggle to reconcile those events that will not leave her, that are "ever-present" in her mind, is balanced against the mute despair of addiction. She describes herself now, at age thirty-five:

> Learning what my addiction was. Starting to learn how to live.
> Met a man. Did volunteer work. Started smoking crack again.
> Feelings getting sorted out. Learning how to work through my
> depressive mind. Starting to really figure out what I want out
> of life. Most of all, started writing this autobiography.

In writing, Gayle is fighting for her life. The very vitality of the words—the innate drive that selects powerful words that stand on their own—demonstrates her keen ear for her own text. Her vocabulary includes words and phrases that are distinctly Biblical. In the spiritual traditions Gayle embraces, human beings are straddling nothing less than the distance between good and evil. Declarations such as "forgive him for he knows not what he's done"—even if applied to a drug-dealing boyfriend—ring with the Gospel message.

Less explicit, perhaps, are the rhythms and phrasings of her sentences, walking between opposite declarations of what she "should" have done and what in fact happened. One such sentence begins:

"When I started drinking, I felt good at what I thought was making love." The thought then winds back into itself with an assessment, a moral accounting of this action: "and I became caught in a world some of us can understand." Her language is soaked in judgment: she relates clearly what she was experiencing, while at the same time insisting on her own condemnation of herself.

The religion practiced and preached her entire life has run on that same parallel design, fashioning startling contradictions that are not, in her mind, contradictions at all. She writes:

> In the beginning, my life was so simple. . . . Though my mother drank and we lived a life of violence, partying, and abuse, we lived traditionally with values and principles and understood that this was our life and we had to live it. We were chosen, and we had to make the best of it.

In these words, two voices compete for the truth. One sees the violence and abusive patterns resulting from alcohol; the other seems to float around it in grim affirmation that she was assigned to that brutal life and had to simply accept it. That these two recollections coexist for her is clear. The consequence seems to be that mute acceptance around which a great deal of her pain clusters, the same inner torment her addiction seeks unsuccessfully to muffle.

GAYLE SELDOM CAME to the dinner program after her assistant position ended. Having gotten a job as a cashier at a local drugstore, she moved from the shelter into her aunt's house in the city. She was moving closer each week to the independent and sober life she wanted and for which she had quit using drugs several months before. She worked hard and constantly, going out only to NA meetings and to work, afraid that her old addictive patterns would prove too tempting if she gave herself too much freedom. The surface of her life was orderly, controlled, and quiet, but her inner life was fraught with anxiety. More than once, Gayle has explained that she needed to work, that it kept her out of mischief by giving her something to do. The painful memories and responsibilities that she had evaded while using drugs grew more and more clamorous in her sobriety.

During this time, Gayle continued to write her story, and we met when we could, in a sort of loose writer-editor relationship. During these meetings, I watched with increasing frustration as her relationships closed down around her. Where before, she had been exuberant, excited to interact with the women at the dinner program, she was now furtive and anxious, often dismissing the company of people she knew. I sensed her withdrawal and her fear. Never relaxed, she smoked in hurried puffs and spoke in short, choppy sentences. Her expression, once so open and radiant, clenched tighter and tighter even when she managed a desperate smile.

"How's work going?" I'd ask.

"Those folks are going to drive me crazy," she'd respond, and smile. "I'm all right, though. I'm all right. It'll be all right."

The store employed her just under full time, so she received no benefits. She stocked items on the shelves and rang purchases up for almost eight hours, five days a week. Because she liked to do her job well, she'd often complete her duties quickly and busy herself with odd jobs. Other employees resented her work ethic, her energetic approach made them look lazy, and the tension increased.

"I just come in, do my job, and leave," she recited. "That's all I'm gonna do anymore."

She wasn't making much money. She didn't spend much time at the dinner program—in part, it seems, because she wanted that part of her life to be firmly in the past. But it turned out that the support, assurance, and social opportunities the program provided were crucial to her maintenance of sobriety. Her austere schedule of simply working at the store then returning home and watching television fostered a painful isolation. In that solitude, her mind played over and over again anthems of depression and worthlessness. Gayle has pride: she wanted this new life to work, for herself, her family, and her children. Yet she grew increasingly terrified of her despair. Like many survivors of trauma, she fought her memories and anxieties as best she could, expecting that will would overcome a lifetime of damage, and failing over and over again because the terror and sadness just wouldn't dissipate.

Occasionally, she would call me at home. In her attempt to sound as if things were going along just fine, I heard the opposite. She cared less about her hair, her dress, the joyless job, the social isolation. She started to spiral into deeper and deeper depression, until she just stopped the pretense.

She left town for a short while, quit the job, and starting using crack again shortly before her first year of sobriety was complete.

THE FIRST TIME I saw her after she was using again was outside the Popeye's Fried Chicken downtown. I was coming from work and she was waiting outside. It was cold and dark and maybe raining. She was standing outside the two glass doors, smoking a cigarette. She might have said, "I thought you forgot me," or "always running late," or something like that. We hugged and walked in.

The smell of grease and buttered biscuits and fast food was as heavy as the exhaust fumes outside. Whitney Houston was singing, "I will always love you," and the cashiers repeated in monotone: Mild or spicy? Light meat or dark meat? What size Coke? Gayle and I got our food and went upstairs where it was quieter. She was talking a mile a minute, but I can't remember what she was saying or what she was wearing. All I could think was: Why's she using now? After so long, why now?

Crack cocaine is cheaper than cocaine. It's the poor folks' drug, though it's not just poor folks that smoke it. At a party once, I listened to an educated, bilingual, middle-class woman describe the lure of crack. How it hits hard and wipes everything out like an eraser on the board. Just a clean sheet across the mind. A short while later, the woman said, you want it again.

"What's it like to smoke crack?" I asked Gayle. "Do you get really happy? Are you suddenly flooded with euphoria?"

She looked at me as if I were the slowest, dullest kid in the class. "You feel nothing," she said. "When I'm high, everything stands still. If I move or talk or anything, I disturb my high. So I don't say anything; I just hold real still."

You.

Feel.

Nothing.

You. The woman that is set apart from the experiences that have made her the woman speaking across the table from me. You, that is, the woman from whom you seek to distance yourself. You, the woman with no memory, no past. Just a body in the moment holding still.

Feel. A dangerous bid. To feel is to fall, to rage and love and have walls and lights come crashing down around, to run away, to be assaulted and raped, to remember, to betray a best friend and to have that friend betray, to get shot in the back, to nearly die.

Nothing. A state of being that is temporarily suspended from feeling or emotion or memory or anything. Precisely why inaction is so necessary. To move is to fail, to feel is to fail, to hold still is to succeed. There is a resonance of the depth of failure to act so deep and implicit in this word that it is almost beyond words.

Gayle is an amazing and sensitive woman, full of instincts and intuition and graceful intelligence. She is socially adept when she wants to be; it's a charm put on and off like an earring. She has a round face and a beautiful smile, flawless and full. She moves with nervous energy, often tapping her finger on the table or shaking her foot while she's waiting for something. Her voice moves quickly and insistently into conversation, and she wants your attention. Or doesn't. It's her choice, and that's what determines her interactions. Yet what undergirds everything I know about her is her relationship with that phrase: You Feel Nothing. Addiction is her lodestar. The recovery rate for crack cocaine is very low.

GAYLE WROTE IN a recent letter from a recovery unit at a local hospital about the beginning of her addiction. I have heard several versions of the same story in the nearly two years I've known her. The story seems to grow a little more distinct in detail each time she tells it, and I wonder if it's because she is coming to a clearer comprehension of her life.

Feminist writer bell hooks believes that autobiography is a thoroughly personal act and that our stories are driven by the need to recover a wholeness that events in lives can shatter. She writes in her book *Talking Back: Thinking Feminist, Thinking Black* about the impact of this written recovery on the present life:

> The longing to tell one's story and the process of telling is symbolically a gesture of longing to recover the past in such a way that one experiences both a sense of reunion and a sense of release. It was the longing for release that compelled the writing but concurrently it was the joy of reunion that enabled me to see the act of writing one's autobiography is a way to find again that aspect of self and experience that may no longer be an actual part of one's life but is a living memory shaping and informing the present.

I would argue that the process is not only symbolic of the act of reconciling a past to a present, but it is for some the means through which we discover the willingness to seek for some deeper unity.

When Gayle writes of her childhood, she has icons of innocence: certain people and events that document a life largely free of addiction, free of the authority an addiction can mandate. Her grandmother, in particular, represents a figure to whom she can return in her mind. When she ran away from home to seek escape from her mother's addictive behavior, she had "somewhere to go. For I ran to Grandma's house and she would be sitting on the front porch and I would sit down and talk to her and she would say that I was in God's hands now and I was going to be all right. . . ." For a powerless child to leave home and have somewhere to go is a saving grace, and it is one for which Gayle is profoundly grateful to this day. For an adult sorting through the wreckage of nearly a lifetime spent under the dictates of addiction, Grandma's porch is just as vital. To recollect something of value is to establish its function in the present; it's an affirmative gesture, a spot of hope. Gayle, in writing out this memory, is reclaiming the possibility that things will be "all right"; she is creating a personal history that allows for survival in the past and the present.

Gayle mailed me an addendum to her story from the hospital. It is important, she wrote, to acknowledge and thank my mother for doing the best she could, for taking in my kids and raising them, for keeping the family together. These recent words testify to the positive actions her mother has taken and for which Gayle is now profoundly grateful. Through Gayle's marriage, divorce, addiction, jail, and recovery, her mother and sister have cared for her five children; they are almost all grown now.

What is impossible to ignore, but what Gayle does not seem to see, is that she herself was neglected as a child. All the time her mother was drinking and partying, when her parents' marriage was falling apart, when her father would disappear onto the road and his return brought further violence, Gayle was a child. Medical researchers and mental health professionals are learning more and more about the inheritance of addictive patterns. Some emphasize its physiological, possibly genetic, nature, while others isolate behavior patterns in family environments. What is evident is that home and kin, through some potent combination, link generation to generation in this legacy of addiction.

In the same way, then, that Gayle's memory retrieves her grandmother's porch as a source of support, it only proves a temporary refuge in the maelstrom of alcoholism and violence. The memories are hard ones that rally against her desperate intentions to believe in, or think she should believe in, a simple life, with "values and principles": even "though my mother drank and we lived a life of violence, partying, and abuse."

Her two narrative voices bang heads in childhood, one declaring the good life with a tricycle and a house like a castle, the other witnessing hard drinking and fights between her mother and often absent father. This essential contradiction in assertions probably mirrors the confusion Gayle felt as a child, when adults acted in ways beyond a child's comprehension. That this tension exists in her adult narrative suggests an emotional blurriness around the harder images, indicates the pain still located around neglect and violence.

Fundamental lessons about safety and trust, about home, about love and respect cross wires throughout her story. This adult's retrieval of what is essentially a child's story tries to resolve the tension by locating the responsibility for pain squarely on the child: "I grew up an angry, resentful, lonely, and hurt child because I couldn't show emotion. I never said to my mother that I loved her. I never showed her I really cared what she said mattered." Her language reveals, even in her adult voice, that the child internalized the rage, confusion, and violence, and it is to this "isolated, self-destructive person" that the adult returns, again and again and again. A cycle of reckless action to gain control over what could not be controlled, to show no mercy and be shown no mercy, to not show emotion, to not care what matters, to not "be a baby." "There was," in her childhood, she says poignantly, "no one to beat me but my mother and father." Her words careen in a frenzied attempt to rationalize her destructive patterns, and land back home.

The source from which she might draw a more complete and forgiving self-portrait is tightly monitored by a fearful obscurity. In her words we hear the self-recrimination that is not the natural property of a child; it is the logic of a child raised to believe that bad things happen because you are bad. The voice reverberates punishingly, without mercy, too frightened to lose the little good by challenging Mother or Father or perceptions of God: the voice seals neatly, holding hostage any awareness of her situation as a child. The phrases that explain this self-destructive path bear the first whisperings of her pain, but they are silenced so effectively and intensified by so much adult pain and violence that it is little surprise the relief is to "feel nothing."

Thanking and absolving her mother are unfortunately misguided by a guilt and confusion so profound they hide the truer voice. Responsibility for past actions slump under the press of absolutist convictions—"taught to be in control"—which are as noisy as they are murky. The long road to recovery is contingent on responding to hard questions: Why did you start using? What do you value most in your life? What can you change? What is beyond your control? Gayle's text is yet blanketed by a fundamental confusion, but her words contain a map for the journey.

I cannot emphasize enough that the dialogue Gayle invents between the telling of her story and her life, and by extension with her private world, would not have been possible without trust. When I share critically what I see in the world her words create, I feel her across the room, even though she is across the city. This autobiography is in many ways her contract with life, and I am one of its trustees. If the truth will set us free, Gayle has asked me to participate in her freedom. She does not harbor illusions about our connection, but this storytelling is an investment nonetheless. She banks words and imagines possibilities against the despair, making me, and each reader in turn, a witness to both.

ALL THE FIVE senses catalogue memory. Some of Gayle's earliest memories are visual: pictures of her grandparents' home and her neighborhood have the effect of still frames from a slide projector. When she moves into adolescence, escorted largely through rape and pregnancy, she shifts the locus of recall into the palpable world, the world of touching and feeling, the world of motion and physical experience. That summer her father did not return to pick her up for a vacation with him, so she spent her fifteenth year with her mother. She wrote recently that "I never wanted to drink because my mother drank and there was always a lot of violent behavior behind it. But this one particular day, a group of my friends got together and bought a bottle of Wild Irish Rose grape wine. We drank it and we felt good. No violent behavior, just a lot of giggles and laughter. . . . When I drink I get drunk and every time I get drunk I want sex."

The shattering cleavage between Gayle's inner and outer lives—severing a relationship between what she perceives, what she desires, and what she experiences—is made manifest by being raped at the age of fifteen. The assault is not only an attack on her desire for intimacy, but it catapults her into adulthood with its resulting pregnancy. The vast majority of rape victims never see their attackers caught, tried, or imprisoned, and one out of every eight adult women has experienced a forcible rape. Rape victims are overwhelmingly female and young; over half are under eighteen. It's impossible to escape the conclusion that sexual assault marks the passage from childhood into adulthood for many women. The fact that it is overwhelmingly underreported, underrated, and untreated is at the heart of a lot of women's silence. The effect on women's lives of the inability to speak of this violence is substance abuse, maladaptive patterns of intimacy, and many other traumatic disorders.

Gayle links the acquaintance rape to alcohol. Her description is sure, quick: "My boyfriend's friend got me drunk and raped me and I got pregnant with my son." Without adornment, its pacing and vocabulary have shorn all but the most essential details from this event. The sparse detail does little justice to the extended impact of the assault. It is the beginning of her relationships with men and her connection to the world of drugs and alcohol and a self-destructive lifestyle.

In *Trauma and Recovery,* Judith Herman explores the belief that:

> The survivor's intimate relationships are driven by the hunger for protection and care and are haunted by the fear of abandonment or exploitation. In a quest for rescue, she may seek out powerful authority figures who seem to offer the promise of a special caretaking relationship. By idealizing the person to whom she becomes attached, she attempts to keep at bay the constant fear of either being dominated or betrayed. . . . Her desperate longing for nurturance and care makes it difficult to establish safe and appropriate boundaries with others.

Gayle's relationship with her husband reverberates between the potential for togetherness and love and "faults"—one of which was infidelity. Gayle invested so much in this relationship that she even "learns to love him unconditionally." This phrasing has religious overtones, suggesting the idealized world she desires; but her fears and his betrayal shatter into confused pieces. The idealism, the love that never dies, grows ragged against the real, and she maintains both the love and the pain in a surreal plunge into drugs. She writes, "My journey into drugs was self-centered tripping because I used it as an excuse and defense to keep my husband away." In other words, she used drugs to ease the fear and pain involved in confronting the sort of dialogue necessary to a more trusting relationship. Such a dialogue would name names, acknowledge rape and abuse, locate responsibility within herself and those she loves.

In this precarious world, Gayle initially avoids prostitution to support her habit and steals instead. The consequence is jail and further distance from her family, especially her children. Gayle's narrative does not reckon in any detailed way with the guilt she feels about the impact drugs had on her ability to care for her children. The Reverend Norma Jennings at the D.C. Correctional Treatment Facility once told me that one of the hardest stages of recovery is to face how addiction betrays children. When a woman comes out of her addiction far enough to understand how she has abandoned her children, it's a decisive moment toward further recovery. Owning up to that responsibility will either snuff her resolve to face the whole truth and she will flee back into narcotics or it will enable the mother to build bridges to a new family. Gayle, in honoring her mother and sister for raising her children and in writing this text, nervously fingers the beginning of this wholly intimate, complex task.

WHEN GAYLE LEFT her childhood home, she moved in with a boyfriend, had a second child with him, and tried to leave him five times until he shoots her. Her response? She writes:

> And my life flashed before my eyes of always getting a whipping from the age of five years to now. Always getting punished for being a bad girl, for something I had done wrong. But I hadn't done anything wrong to die for that night. So I got up and sat on the step and told him, I forgive you. But I will never forget what he had done.

This is the voice of her addiction. Its eye is vital and immediate, its ear canny. The bad girl echo resounds: everything bad that happens is somehow punishment meted out from beyond her control. It is the voice of absolutes, a fixed universe in which her power is extremely limited. Yet there is the persistence to endure, a shard of will glimmering, however imprecisely, in the words "but I hadn't done anything wrong to die for that night," followed by the resolution in the forgiveness reflex, the clutch toward some kind of justice.

Writing as part of recovery, as well as writing for its own sake, resists the passivity endemic to addiction. In telling her story, Gayle takes on the massive silence that cloaks her deepest terrors and failures, but also contains the key to a sober and peaceful future. Her autobiography will not carry her effortlessly from addiction into recovery, but she has generated an authentic voice for her struggle. Gayle speaks against the silence one word, one page, one day at a time.

FOUR

"I'M STAYING DOWN HERE
WHERE IT'S BIZARRE"

Ann

At thirteen, I boarded a plane headed for Izmir, Turkey. I got rid of my dog and went to another country first-class. I wore a blue denim, rhinestone-studded outfit. It was the only time I related to my parents because we were on a spiritual plane.

The Turkish economy was poor, and yet my parents made friends with a rich man named Arief. He was the Onassis of Turkey. He took us to his property and I hung out with my parents' friends. They were always drinking and so I got drunk on some ozu. I got mononucleosis and I was sick for two weeks but I really think it was from the hash I smoked. My best friend was a Japanese-American named J. We were so cool in our school and at dances. I would look funny and out of place because I came from an uncaring and nonloving alcoholic home. My father would give me an order and expect everyone to obey. He would take trips and bring back Greek rugs and buy a lot of copper and brass from the market. He also would buy film for his movie camera. He worked for NATO and when we would go to the beach he would have to call off the trip when his walkie-talkie went off. We would all have to go to church even though Catholic mass meant nothing to us. I enjoyed the hot sun and walking around the ruins in Ephesus.

When I returned to this country, everyone noticed how exotic I looked in high school. They really noticed I had been somewhere. I had bracelets all up my arm and I didn't understand why everyone wasn't cool. Instead I found snobbiness. All the girls wore Farrah Fawcett feathered-back hair and I missed my friends in Turkey. I was the girl everyone saw as wild and yet the teachers admired me. I could do anything.

Now I'm homeless, and the psychiatrists have labeled me as manic-depressive. In other words, they say I have mood-swings. I don't know how my mood has anything to do with having been experienced in the universe, but I know who I am. I was a straight-A and -B student throughout college. I'm about as consistent as they come and I grow tired of being put in with women who are ill. It's crazy. I've never had much money but I've always depended on the government, having a military ID all my life. But I'm certainly not a mood-swinger. I want to travel again and see other countries such as Turkey.

When I was in college, I met a guy. I had such a crush on him. His name was W. M. I saw it on his timecard in the library on the second floor. We would sort books and talk. I think about him almost every day because time moved so quickly and separated us. I remember the moment that he kissed my hand and we sat together at the telephone cafe. In the cafe, we talked in the red atmosphere where tiny red telephones were on every table. Outside, the blizzard snow blew. He said that he was worried about me and asked where I lived. And I was afraid that the cops were going to wreck my home. I should have told him about it but I couldn't, not then, because another cop had busted into my apartment for no reason and I was also raped by a black guy named Anthony. The rape was during a thunderstorm and now I am sorry and I miss W. M. and I can not change the way I behaved.

I just couldn't hold it together. When W. M. told me that he was leaving for Prague, I followed him. Some rich Texan named S. at an AA meeting gave me the money. I loved Europe, but I couldn't find W. M. without an address or phone number.

Then I made a mistake and flew back to Portland from Prague. It

looked so weird—log trucks and pine trees. I left a happy world in
Europe for the deep mystery of Oregon. I ended up in a small town
called Burns. In Burns, it was as if I ran into the devil himself, it was
like something was chasing me, and I called my dad and told him
so. He wired me money for a Greyhound and he met me at the station. I felt like the slot machines had demons in them, and Dad told
me that he saw the devil in the sky in Vietnam.

Coming home from Europe is rough. You're in such a beautiful
place and return to such a cold empty place. Why? Why return here?
There are so many gaps between people. In Germany there are
approximately 650 people per square mile. Here there are approximately 25 people per square mile. We have a strange culture
between buildings and street people, and the crime continues to
climb. That's why I like foreign countries. In Mexico, I noticed how
everything is tilted in line with the $23\frac{1}{2}°$ axis the earth sits on.
Americans try to keep everything straight when it's usually not.

IN A MIAMI church I had once found a strange statue of Jesus. For
some reason the figure seemed to open and close his mouth like a
dripping wax figure. He seemed to say, "Help me, help me." The
church was overall not that interesting compared to some of the
Mexican churches I have been in. Guadalajara Jalico: there was an
altar that had a certain hand instead of a cross. An alien hand bent
in an off-world fashion. The darkness of the ciudad like a black
vague glove that covers the city of cathedrals where dogs stand
guard on top of houses.

I answered an ad for a woman who was lonely for a live-in companion. She was a Mexican spinster who lived inside the twinkling
of the city on Elocial Parra avenue. She called herself "The War-
wick" and I remember her grey hair. She let me in and explained
that she was looking for a live-in companion that she could help out.
When I was standing at her doorway in my cowboy boots, she could
see that I needed a place to sleep so she offered me her couch. She
never married nor had any children she explained to me in her mysterious Mexican accent. She would talk about going to Zacatecas

in a few days to see her brother. Her brother had an inflated prostate, so he would constantly be in need of the bathroom.

The young couple visiting was Mexican and American. The husband was a cop from L.A. There was also a grandson there, and he had a baby boy from a wife in El Salvador. That gave me an eerie feeling because when he got up in the night the grandson looked like Elvis Presley attending to a sad baby that had no mother since she was shot in their war.

Once inside the house in Guadalajara, we watched scary Mexican hospital movies and I b.s.'ed with the cop.

"I'm going back to where it's real tomorrow," he said.

"I'm staying down here where it's bizarre," I said as I watched Raul Valasco introduce Alexander Guzman on a Mexican rock show.

Also in Guadalajara, I found a strange group of theater directors who were sitting in an auditorium. They were moving quickly and they introduced themselves while I let them photograph me because I seemed mysterious to them. They seemed surprised that I knew so much about Mexico, telling them all about the pink tiles and gondola in Zacatecas. The gondola goes across the entire city. I had a feeling that these directors were extraterrestrials because one introduced himself as Octopus. I never saw them again.

I met another group of theater people in Guadalajara where we watched Veronica Castro every night. This was during the Gulf War, and for some reason it felt as if bombs were dropping or some creature was on the roof every night. That's just how Guadalajara felt—as if a creature was on the roof. There was also another day when I was by a swimming pool and I imagined a group of large stingrays swimming around in a sulfur water pool.

Mexico can become surreal. They say that diablo is real and I saw a tiny fish in Mazatlan that was indeed called a devilfish. They call him the Lobos and his face is that of a wolf and his body is of a sea creature. Mazatlan is a beautiful city where I sailed to from La Paz in Baja, California. I had no idea that I would find a circus in Mazatlan. While in La Paz, I poured perfume down my neck from a bottle shaped like a cat. I set sail the next day across the channel. The bottle seemed magical because I found ten live cats at the circus. They were tigers. And they were beautiful. I traveled with Union Circo to the city of Culican in Sin Aloa, Mexico. I met my boyfriend Martin there. Mexicans are fun because they all like to pile in places together. Martin was tall, dark, and handsome, and I swear his city was long and narrow where all the cars have blackened their windows and everyone hangs out at the funeral parlor waiting for the next event while they eat tortillas. Their funerals are real because I've attended a few. They pack the nose with salt and bury the person the next day. Death is a common event in Mexico and they have no budget for embalming. American funerals are different from any other countries. Ours are done privately and secretly while theirs are out in the open. There are many graveyards and many white crosses. I am sorry to report that I was not in the country for the day of the dead.

IN THE MIRROR I looked as I was being arrested in Chetumal, Mexico. I had no other item but the mirror. I held it in my hand and recited a prayer from the fiery pit that burned all around me. The Spanish voices of police who refused to speak to me. It was not clear as to what they had planned. In the distance was a Chinese circus. Just outside the window of light. Time became endless as I sat in a chair where clouds passed outside as if not connected to the people underneath.

Once at the jail, I saw rain showering down, and I felt hunger during the time of my arrival that I would never forget. My bed was the cement ground and in the distance were boys playing soccer and painting piñata. Female hands searched my body for various objects. Then she put me in a cell where water was being brought in large buckets. She then again appeared at my jail cell, smoking and wearing my clothes. More rain in the jail that was overlooking a tropical Cancún garden. There, tenderness in the music we listened to as we hung in our hammocks and experienced being in jail. I smuggled a rug between my bars with a note I slipped to Anthony. The voices I heard at night were of other people calling out to forgotten loved ones who were not there. I heard a man calling, "Veronica, Veronica." His grief was in the shadows of the endless night where my time ended in three days and I was flown to Miami via Mexican Air.

It was 1992 or '93 when I was in Miami, and I was a beach bum, artist, and looked for work. One night, I was sleeping at the church or rather a dome-shaped Jewish temple dedicated to Anne Frank where I would watch and wait for the old bearded white male Jews to lock up. At that time, I had been homeless for about a month. I slept under the pinkish-orange, hot Miami skies until one night a silver-haired, tall, and thin policeman drove up and appeared in the starlit twilight. As he came toward me through the dreamy Miami mist, I noticed the smirk on his clean-shaven face. He wanted to know where my husband was. I informed this navy blue-uniformed stranger that I did not have one. He noticed my rhinestone earrings lying next to my pillow and my black briefcase full of scripts. The scripts were for a television show I had filmed at the Shawnee Hotel where I read a war story I had written during a thunderstorm one night. That night, a stray cat was my only friend.

IN 1993, I joined the military. While I was in a Florida boot camp, I was called down to the officer in charge.

"It says here that you were standing naked with shaving cream all over your body," the officer accused.

"I did not," I responded. "I'll have you know that I have religion."

"This is the military. What does religion have to do with this?"

I felt like it was a useless case. I was practically kneeling in front of him. Boot camp was stupid.

I have a friend, a D.C. cop, who said all the trouble that I had in boot camp was because of their sexual discrimination. So maybe I did have shaving cream all over my body. They gave me the can when I went in. Just because some dumb girl went and told doesn't make me an idiot. It makes her a perverted little peeping Tom. Why was she looking at me in the shower in the first place? It was because of this incident that I was pushed into psychology and dealing with military shrinks over some shaving cream. Then they had to research my whole life, including my childhood and not to mention various inkblot tests and they hooked probes to my head to listen to the electrons. The truth is I could not survive in a company where men and women were integrated. No sir, when the company commander said that he wanted all the girls to lock up their bras in the lockers and hand in all tampons. Like we were no longer free women! He was crazy. The bras belong with the rest of the clothes in the bag. As for tampons, I'm not asking no man permission for a tampon when it's my time of the month. I got booted out of there because I was already on my period and when one of the girls took me aside for having a string hanging out of my p.t. [exercise] shorts, I said, "That doesn't matter, they're boys, they can handle it. I mean we're all supposed to be troops so they can get used to the sight of blood a little early." They locked me up in solitary confinement for that.

His name was Captain X. He was my doctor in the psych ward at boot camp. He shook my hand like a dead fish. And he was so old and tall like a statue. A scar ran through his face. He was Polish and he was in World War II. I think he was a Burghermeister, the torturer of children, during the war. Now he has a new power of counseling the minds of military personnel and pushing psychotropic drugs.

The military was so strange, I thought. Sometimes I felt that Captain X was a vampire, as he would walk into the rooms having everyone fear him because he had been in the past of Germany. He was a real Nazi. He would sit and listen intensely to young enlisted recruits' sob stories of how they wanted out of the military because they were not happy or why they had tried to commit suicide. He would lambaste the recruits with so much terror that the recruits would sink into their chairs or shoot up out of their seats and struggle to fight. He always used that "Father Knows Best" method of verbal punishment and then would be forced to recommend a discharge or threaten a court-martial.

I was at the psych ward for six months. I would sit next to Dr. X to be daring. Some of the patients were quickly drawn into involving themselves in relationships with other patients. Cookie paired off with B., an old torpedo man, whose wife caused him to hurt himself. Cookie was a short blond who arrived at the hospital with her feet tied at her ankles. She was a stripper and her father was a police chief. Cookie would cry and fight with another patient, Arnold, while I continued to wear my dungarees and feel like a fat man encased in prison clothing.

Once Cookie and I had a good time joking around inside the dreary hospital. Inside our rooms we had hospital beds, a sink with no mirror, a shower, and a toilet. We couldn't have a mirror because we were on a psych ward, and mirrors can be tools for cutting yourself if they are broken. There was a hallway that led past the bedrooms; all had bedspreads, white with the mental hospital look. All the orderlies were in whites that squeaked clean of tidiness. And although we knew we were locked up, we still sang songs like Cookie's favorite, "Somewhere Over the Rainbow," but all the songs sounded faded and blue. Outside, the Florida sun was hot, and the traffic slow-moving. Yet a wonderful pond was just outside the window to add to our boot camp atmosphere.

I sat and survived the torture of having almost all my privileges taken away. My hair was brown and scraggly, and I had outgrown my uniforms. The hospital staff brought in some mats for me to exercise on, but it didn't work. I was still fat. At times, they would take me out for walks. They made sure to issue suntan lotion in case I burned, but I felt more like a kewpie doll than a human being. The best exercise I received was when we played volleyball outside. The doctors dressed out and played with us too. I gave one doctor a warning telling him that the court made out of sand was less dangerous than the one made of asphalt but he didn't listen. Later he twisted his ankle on the asphalt court and another doctor had to take him home.

While I was in the hospital, I felt so degraded. That is how you begin to feel—like a nobody, like you have no rights and you become the property of the military. One of the things I remember is that I saw things that were not right. People taking psychotropic drugs such as melodril for personality disorders instead of actual psychological breakdowns. One guy was given lithium for urinating on the sidewalk. I said, "So did Billy Carter," and they said, "Shhh!"

There was a woman named Miss Julie who was a knockout in her theater-white hair that looked stunning late at night as she sat on the navy blue couch while thunderstorms outside flashed and flickered. I fantasized about spraying her hair with glitter and sparkle hair spray as if she were a goddess. One night, we had to do group therapy in the hallway. Miss Julie was to direct the session. The topic that night was "What Is Proper Behavior and What Is Not?" The whole thing came about because Cookie talked excessively about sex and so all of us had to participate in the session. At the time, I was more concerned about how I was going to leave the hospital because Captain X had said I had to go medevac strapped to a gurney. There was a guy there from Michigan who insisted to Miss Julie that I should be able to just walk out instead of being on a gurney. He played up to her and complimented her by calling her the nickname "White Swan" because she always wore an emblem or a piece of small jewelry with a swan on it. My friend from Michigan would say things like "Wow, the White Swan," and then he would whistle and tell her she was pretty hot. After he beefed her up with compliments, he hit her with the question of how I was going to leave the hospital. I was so glad someone finally cared, because for whatever reason, I felt like if I left the hospital on a gurney, I was going to die.

After the plane landed, I was taken to the military base. All the beds at Bethesda were full, so I had to wait at Andrews in the company of several camouflaged soldiers. The interior of the room was a pale green and I thought it resembled a morgue. I was so cold from the air conditioning, and I slept in the cold until someone turned it off. Soon I was moved to Bethesda where I met my roommate, M. She was a woman who was being given shock therapy. She informed me that her husband was a NASA employee before he died and that she had over two hundred thousand dollars.

My lawyer, Lt. V., was a young lady who didn't care about my case. My time in court went fast, and afterwards a nurse put me in a room and kept saying "the diagnosis" over and over again. Then I had to go into another room where all these strange people who were not in uniform said that I was mentally ill. This ordeal they called "rounds." I was then taken into a room and told by a blond nurse that I was caught in a web and that I had to return to Florida on a gurney. I then dismissed myself and went to Sunday mass.

This is when I went AWOL for over a year. I had been living in a shelter and one day Miss B. found my AWOL status on her computer. I rode with the cops, was cuffed and taken to the airport in Washington, D.C., where I encountered two military personnel whom I had to follow. I went back to Florida in handcuffs on USAir. When we got to Florida, we got in a private car and we got lost. They turned to me and asked for directions. I was in the back seat and I said that I didn't know, gosh. We had to ask someone how to get to the base. Once back at my command, I said goodbye to them, hung out in the barracks, and went to chow with a chaser (another recruit about nineteen years old). This lasted until a fight broke out with the adults and I was thrown into an ambulance all because I objected to the Mini-Moe. Mini-Moe is jogging in place with a gun and screaming at the boy to Do it etc. So I ended up back in the hospital.

Without mirrors, I felt the sudden lack of intimacy, while all around I felt the strange feeling of fog. To be caught in an orb cloud of pressurized gas and I was the ancient ruin. A relic of historical data. Once back in the hospital, I said hello to all my old enemies. I slept until morning after giving blood to Miss Z, the other nurse from India. Doctor X was gone. He mysteriously disappeared.

Since I had left the psych ward, things were less structured, the outcome of what I went through had changed. There was no more doctor's group and I felt more certain for my survival. The evil "Oman" was gone.

I had to wrestle more with the bull from the new doctor though. He told me that my check would only be a piece of paper because I had no identification, and I told him that the military had a responsibility to cash my check. And I was right. I got paid and discharged on November 4th, 1994.

I found it funny that the military psychiatrists tend to shut things up when anything metaphysical is mentioned. War is a heavy load on the conscience. Modern drugs have flaws and serious side effects, but we must understand ourselves in order to maintain order. They say the war in Russia and in Yugoslavia is run by Radovan Karadzic, who is a clinical psychiatrist. There, we see a situation that does not have any understanding of their life's purpose. A sad venture into the human soul where the mind, heart, and conscience are shattered by the brutal weapons of survival. Someday I would like to work with the shellshocked victims of today's war and also with individuals diagnosed with mental illness. This is because I see that most young individuals are like tiny undeveloped eggs—fragile and in need of emotional Band-Aids. I do not like labels such as "mentally ill" or "manic-depressive" or even "schizo." We are condemning one another instead of understanding each other on a greater metaphysical level. I am an artist and I wish to learn all I can in the field of investigating.

NOW ALL I want is to be back in the military. Now I'm a civilian woman lost in another dimension. I want to be accepted into the military, but they have a rigid format based on a culture I didn't agree with. I can't see living a civilian life when in the military you have much more. Much more. I had such an exhilarating feeling coming off the plane and sitting in the rooms with all military personnel. It's a high that you can never forget. And I read about our troops all the time in places like Haiti and dream about going. I dream about being in Cuba and solving some problems over there in the Miami area. It's so interesting.

To be in the military is like being a god—more freedom and a greater freedom. And all the items that I wanted, tattoos and jewelry and my uniform that they took away. It was all mine, and it is mean how they took it all away. I planned on going to interesting places and receiving rank and honors. But I got all sidetracked in the hospital and everyone forgot me. Or the doctors were too hung up on mental illness and what happened in Oregon and so they dumped all my dreams and everything I dreamed of was lost and ripped into pieces by others.

DISCUSSION

Deborah Pugh

$\mathcal{A}$nn sees the world as a mysterious place full of aliens, mystical symbols, and forces beyond our immediate senses. As an individual and a writer, she seems to tip the scales of perceivable reality, casting her imaginative net as ancient goddesses did in enchanted forests or forbidden caves. Ann's manic-depressive illness grants her glimpses into the murky unconscious and the realm of imagination. Yet while her own kind of creativity shapes both her writing and her life, it also opens both to what may be the harsh judgments of others. At the same time, her writing reveals the poignancy of her frustrated desire for someone to help her and a place to belong.

I first met Ann on a frigid Tuesday morning in February 1995. Although seeing white women in the shelter was not unusual, Ann tended to stand out in any crowd. Jet black dye covered her cropped hair, gelled to stand in uneven clusters wild and free of convention. Rainbow glitter splashed across her forehead and over her blue-shadowed lids. Her eyes—highlighted by bold Egyptian-like lines that forked out almost to her temples—were that day both exotic and knowing. I had seen Ann several times at Rachael's House, but typically she simply sat reading the *Washington Post* in one of the brown vinyl chairs in the living room and had never joined my writing class. On this particular morning, she had taken a space at the wooden table in front of the windows and was reading *Flying Saucers: A Modern Myth* by Carl Jung.

"Are you a Jung fan?" I asked, hoping to draw her out.

She answered with an "uh?" and a "yeah." Hardly what I had expected, but one thing I had learned about the habits of homeless women was that conversation between strangers was not commonplace. Talk was rare unless a program was initiating the interaction, a card game was in progress, or the women already knew each other. It was seldom discontent or animosity that caused the women to sit in their chairs, silent and withdrawn; it was more likely to be their weary resistance to yet more inquiring questions from strangers or near-strangers or their fear of the consequences of innocently divulged information. To stay in overnight shelters was to expect the worst: fellow residents barking in the middle of the night, women dying in the shower, thieves hatching plots to steal anything from money to the most precious possessions—a driver's license or identification card. Even used underwear was not secure from the stranger in the next bed.

One of the few characteristics Ann shared with the other homeless women was her suspiciousness and emotional distance from volunteers who entered the shelter. In fact, her tendency to be reserved was a product of experience, both from her childhood and her contact with mental health professionals. Although she was well aware that any behavior or conversation might be construed as pathological, she had developed, to my amazement, a casual acceptance and frank acknowledgment of it most of the time. In our many conversations, I was reminded again and again of a terrible dream in which I had been locked in a mental institution. The dream-me protested, calmly and logically, that there was a mistake, but as I told the note-taking attendants that I was not crazy, they would shake their heads and inform me that just by uttering these words I had proved that I was.

My dream represented the unnerving dilemma, the catch-22, of mental illness that Ann faced. I felt sometimes that if Ann were a famous writer or artist, any attempt to distinguish whether she was

mentally ill or simply eccentric would be shrugged off, if not celebrated. But everything about her—including her delight in wearing
purple wigs, layers of scarves and rhinestones, and exotic clothing—
was seen by shelter staff and other homeless women as signs of dis-
turbance rather than marks of individuality.

Understanding Ann, however, required getting past labels and
assumptions. I am not a therapist and must resist the temptation to
make any assessment of Ann's mental state based on my interactions
with her as her friend and writing teacher. Yet I will say that, during our five months of working together, I never witnessed any out-
ward manifestations of mental illness, although at times I saw her
try to deliberately shock other homeless women and staff with her
stories and behavior. For example, she told about a healer in the
Adams-Morgan neighborhood of Washington who was rearranging
the energy fields of her body with magnets and crystals. Ann was
very concerned because she had had to leave in the middle of the
treatments due to lack of money, and she feared that the healer had
set something awry that was affecting the way she felt. I knew that,
for some, this type of treatment was a valid alternative medical practice, so when she told me about it, I asked if she had discussed it
with anyone else. She said she had told her psychiatrist and the shelter staff because she thought they should know about other thera-
pies she was exploring. When I asked what the psychiatrist said, she
replied that he scribbled a lot of notes and changed her prescription.

Another situation illustrates how the most innocuous of actions
could be perceived as bizarre when it came to Ann. As usual, when
I arrived that morning, most of my regulars were waiting to have
class; however, Ann was not there. Her absence was unusual
because she had never missed class before, but when I asked about
her, a staff member told me that she had been expelled from
Rachael's for the day because of trouble during breakfast. The story
was that Ann had come to the shelter early for coffee and a donut.
After she finished her donut, she began to blow bubbles in her coffee through the stirring stick. Completely engrossed in the process
of blowing bubbles, Ann didn't notice that one of the women at her

table had gone to the kitchen to complain that Ann's actions were making her sick at her stomach. When a staff person asked Ann to stop, she responded with a mild expletive. I attributed this ill temper to the morning hour because I had never heard Ann utter a curse word. But the staff member tried to explain the incident by saying, "Maybe Ann has stopped her medication and she's 'acting out.'"

To compensate for the lack of companionship at the shelter, Ann haunted the Martin Luther King Memorial Library, free movies at the Smithsonian, museums, and various off-beat stores. One day, she took me to one of her favorite shops, La Botica, in the Adams-Morgan district. When walking down Columbia Road, you feel as if you have crossed a conceptual border into Central and South America. Canopies and backdrops are hitched to unsteady frames, and foldup tables on sidewalks display cheap watches, boom-box batteries, oranges and mangoes, audiotapes, and clothing. Vendors scream out, "Señora, Señorita," while women with swathed babies watch the people passing by. Through this throb of life, Ann and I entered the smudged glass door that led upstairs to La Botica.

It was like stepping out of place and time. A woman stood, motionless and not particularly welcoming, behind a glass case containing bulk herbs and extracts. To her left was a tiny room where two old, sun-beaten Hispanic men wearing straw cowboy hats and boots were staring into space. Ann whispered, "Curanderos. Healers. Shamans. You can consult with them, but it costs a lot of money." Two gigantic altars dominated the store. One was an almost life-size statue of Jesus from the waist up. In the basin in his lap were hundreds of quarters, fifty-cent pieces, and folded notes containing wishes and requests. Clothespinned to every part of his upper torso were hundreds of dollar bills, creating giant fans of greenbacks like leis. His sad eyes and drops of blood on his tilted head rimmed with thorns seemed to cry out to supplicants who came to ask forgiveness, to pray for prosperity, or to make an offering. The other altar, a retable, displayed morose carved saints, their eyes searching heaven for answers. Bundles of flowers, burning candles, and bits of cloth with images of the Virgin Mary or Jesus were cluttered around the retable. Coexisting with these altars were shelves and shelves of candles to ward off evil spirits, elixirs to dispel evil spirits after bodily invasion, and herbs and powders to place spells on irritating neighbors. I could see why Ann loved this place. It projected deep into the heart of mystery, delving into a collective unconscious.

By contrast, the tedium of homeless life did not offer Ann much in the way of stimulation. She also struggled with the effects of medication that dulled her senses, causing her to miss the edge of immediate experience that she sought. Many times I felt that experience must have exploded into Ann, bypassing the conscious framework of cognition and landing directly in the senses and unconscious. I always felt that Ann knew the difference between reality and her imagination, but her imaginative space was more exciting, more inviting, and far more secure than the lifeless reality she experienced. Perhaps purple wigs and bohemian outfits block our ability to see the hopes and dreams of other people. Ann dreamed about the time she would become the artist of her life again and regain what she desperately missed—intellectual challenges, companionship, love, and above all, mystery.

AT THE HEART of creativity is making the familiar in some way strange or making the strange familiar. This process shakes us out of our cognitive ruts, permitting new perspectives on the phenomenon of life. Embedded in this psychic "stuff" of writers are the imagination and the lived experience, one anchored in the other. However, *how* imagination and lived experience anchor in or relate to each other touches the heart of Ann's writing and her engagement with the world around her. Whether it was a conscious decision for Ann to favor the unconscious and the imagination over lived experience, I cannot say, but her writing does suggest that when desire is strong, imagination can dominate memory.

My primary job in working with Ann as a writer was to piece together and provide chronology and transition to her work. Ann did not view plot as this happened and, consequently, that happened. For her, events just occurred in bits and pieces, without a causality that she could either deduce or confront. Organizing her writing was therefore no easy task and finally could be resolved only by my sitting down with her to get dates for the fragments of autobiographical writing she submitted in class. I truly believe Ann had full command of her memory. However, there are significant gaps in both her writing and her memory, as well as an apparently conscious reluctance to divulge memories of childhood. I got the feeling from our brief conversations about her early life that it may have included isolation and abuse. If so, that may have accounted for the many times Ann could have written about childhood experiences in our writing exercises but did not. On the few occasions when she did, her exploration was superficial.

The power of Ann's writing was not to be found in the revising stage because she absolutely refused to rewrite. During writing class, as soon as my explanation of an exercise was complete, she would begin freewriting furiously, filling two pages for every paragraph of the more contemplative writers in class. Remarkably enough, the mental processes and language configuration were just as apparent in her speech as in her writing. Ann's rejection of introspection and contemplation in her creative inner world resulted in language rendered as close as possible to unconscious experience.

In life as in literature, a reader comes to know characters in a story through the decisions they make in a conflict. But what is strikingly absent from Ann's writing is her emotional reactions to the conflicts she finds herself in. And there were many. From our talks and some of her writing, I could tell that her parents caused her considerable distress as a child. Her father she describes as authoritarian, her mother domineering and threatening; both apparently drank excessively. Consequently, Ann's life as a child was chaotic, often isolated, and terribly unpredictable. In response to an exercise in which I asked the class to write a history of a scar, Ann wrote about the day her mother was drunk and tried to run over her with the car. Although she indicated that this event changed her life, she did not explore the emotional turmoil it caused. She did not want to consider *why* it changed her life. Instead she wrote about a scar on her mother's knee that Ann believed represented a device planted there by aliens to make earthlings destroy other earthlings. When I asked her if she really believed that, she mumbled, "It could happen." I felt overwhelmed by the amount of pain Ann must have experienced as a little girl to concoct such an explanation.

In Ann's writings, this absence of articulated emotional conflicts, whether external or internal, creates more of a character sketch than a true characterization of herself. It seems almost impossible to know a character who is so detached from events in the text. To be fair to Ann, I do not know whether this omission was an unconscious decision, a deliberate choice to conceal her emotions out of a desire for privacy, or some other reason.

Nevertheless, all emotions are not hidden in the text, even if they are yet unrealized by Ann, the writer. In her writing, we see that whenever she is in emotional turmoil, the external world she perceives becomes foggy, dark, mysterious, and above all, more surreal. Time stretches into timelessness, while sensory images flash like lightning bolts. Fear or extreme emotion seems to cause her to shrink from the conscious and give free play to the unconscious. Her arrest in Mexico—which was for not having proper identification—must have been terrifying for her, the last in a series of horrible incidents in which she was first raped by men in a truck and then robbed of her pocketbook, which included her money and identification papers. She begins her memory of the arrest scene with "in the mirror I looked . . . [and] recited a prayer from the fiery pit that burned all around me." Voices of police swirl in the air while Ann looks out "the window of light," for "time became endless as I sat in a chair where clouds passed outside as if not connected to the people underneath." Female hands, seemingly unattached, search her body while children shout, the circus plays in the distance, and tender music floats into the window of light. Voices moan for loved ones in the darkness of "shadows of endless night."

Visualizing this scene is nightmarish, as image upon image

flashes over Ann. The fiery pit, the prayer, and the window of light frame the emotional struggle in somewhat Biblical or Jungian symbolism. She is consumed in the flames of her fears, and like all symbolic fire, she can either be transformed or destroyed by it. To gain control, she uses a prayer, a vocal incantation. This is the mouth of fire as it is defined in the collective unconscious: using speech, the creative force, as a weapon against the fire. Symbolically, speech is an intermediate point between the internal and external worlds, and Ann's utterings into the fiery pit serve to bring the torrent of emotions under control. The odd phrasing of the "window of light" creates the image of sunlight flooding through so powerfully that the physical window disappears and only acts as an opening for illumination.

When Ann is returned to the psychiatric ward after going AWOL in the Army, again her deep-felt emotions find expression in symbols of the unconscious. She writes, "Without mirrors, I felt the sudden lack of intimacy while all around I felt the strange feeling of fog. To be caught in an orb cloud of pressurized gas and I was the ancient ruin. A relic of historical data." Instead of release from the fiery pit, Ann seems to feel the world pushing on her, suffocating her. Again, vision is obstructed by fogginess, and the atmosphere presses in on her until she sees herself as an ancient ruin, a relic, left decrepit and devoid of people and life.

This use of a mirror is common in Ann's autobiographical writings. In traditional symbolism, the mirror has been thought of as a symbol of the imagination, the consciousness, and thought. Our long fascination with mirrors comes from their ability both to reflect the outer world and, in some conceptions, to magically absorb and hold images to be used for future conjuring. When Ann is arrested in Mexico, she recites her prayer into the mirror, yet when she is readmitted into the psychiatric ward for the second time, she feels the loss of intimacy without mirrors. From knowing Ann, I think she uses the mirror as a door, the moving passage between her conscious and unconscious. The mirror could also represent her conscious self, in that she commands its allegiance in jail and yearns for its existence in the psychiatric ward. It is as if looking in the mirror reaffirms her existentially. She is a being in the time and space of the outer world, and although trapped in her inner worth, she becomes aware that even there is conscious existence.

IN HER WRITING, Ann seems to be struggling to find coherence among the archetypal female images of Superwoman, the Exotic Experienced Goddess, and the Powerless Victim Caught in a Web. Negotiating among these three requires one or a combination of the following memory strategies: repress or "forget" the specific memories that cause the intense psychic pain; live in the imagination of a desirable idealized self; or live in the temporal moment, only remembering in sensory glimpses without attention to cause and effect. I believe Ann used elements of all three.

In fact, if Ann's autobiographical story takes a shape, it is one of the hero's mythological quest to solve the antithetical elements in her life. Her writing reveals the tension of attraction and repulsion in the human soul. When she is young, she leaves with her parents for Turkey, where she says she grows up. It is the first leg of the journey in which she wrestles to merge herself as the Exotic Experienced Goddess, who is wild and cool and can do anything, with the awkward girl from an "uncaring and nonloving alcoholic home." As Ann leaves her home and family to attend college, she embarks into the world beyond her parents' influence. In college, she makes good grades, but apparently lacks direction until she jets off to Europe to find her romantic hero, W. M. Failure marks the endeavor, and the Goddess returns and becomes the Powerless Victim Caught in a Web for the first time.

Again, there are many gaps to the story. We do not know how long she was in Europe or how she supported herself while she was there. But it seems that this period—although she fell short of finding her prince—was a time of mastery. The Exotic Experienced Goddess had taken the leap without any resources other than those she possessed and succeeded in breaking into the world. But it was also the beginning of her first breakdown.

Then, after her first hospitalization in Oregon, Ann is able to break free and inhabit her Goddess role again. The language in her writing about her travels to Mexico is original and evocative; it powerfully captures the strange and colorful ambiance that I've also felt in Mexico. There, Ann descends into the mystery of another culture—one in which the dark mysteries of the unconscious are saturated not with fear but with fascination and stimulation.

All bodes well until the tremendous psychic forces clash again and she joins the military. It was always curious to me why someone creative, rebellious, and headstrong like Ann would want to be part of an authoritarian, hierarchical organization like the military. She talks in her writing about the travel, uniform, benefits, and sense of belonging that appeal to her. But is there more? Perhaps Ann—still in conflict over her subjugation to her father, the military man—does not choose the path to self-actualization by separating into independence; rather she joins forces with authoritarianism, believing that by associating with those in power, she will be allowed to wield the power of Superwoman.

ANN'S WRITING, STREWN with metaphor, reflects the way she experiences the world. Separated from threatening emotions in her real self, Ann's life in some sense *is* metaphor—like the flashing images that come to us in dreams. Was her writing all rich metaphor, revealing its own deeper patterns and authentic connections? Some readers may feel it is sometimes simply gibberish—random, incoherent rantings in which even the most creative approach can find no pattern or explanation. However, the more I became familiar with Ann's work, the more I believed that before me was someone who was as close to precognitive thinking as I had ever met. Here was a person who had eliminated similes from her thinking and vocabulary. If a person or object suggested certain characteristics, then that person or object was not "like" something else: rather, the person or object was the thing itself.

For instance, Ann wrote about Captain X, the psychiatrist in the mental ward, "He was Polish and he was in World War II. I think he was a Burghermeister, the torturer of children, during the war. . . . I felt that Captain X was a vampire as he would walk into the rooms having everyone fear him because he had been in the past of Germany. He was a real Nazi." When Ann gave me this piece of writing, I asked if she really believed the doctor was a vampire and a Nazi. After some nudging, she laughed and said, of course, she did not, but he did seem that way to her at the time. She even brought me a picture of the actor Martin Landau from a movie in which he was a demonic warlock to show me what Captain X looked like.

Although this type of thinking and its construction in language challenge our normal modes of cognition and communication, acknowledging it is essential to understand Ann's writing and, ultimately, her view of the world. She knows consciously that Captain X is not a vampire or a Nazi; but deep in her psyche, he represents what is most horrendous to her: Nazis, vampires, and torturers of children. Whether the lack of explicit comparisons results from the projection of her deepest fears or from linguistic peculiarities attributable to manic-depression, I don't know. But this characteristic suffuses her writing, haunting her language with an eerie, surreal quality.

The same archetypal depiction seemed to surround the Greys, the aliens who pop into her narratives at will. In her song about Johnny, the alien Greys come to this lonely boy offering him escape from Earth to realize his dreams.

Untitled Song

Hey hey Johnny hey hey. Why don't you ever go out and play?
Hey hey Johnny hey hey.

Johnny lives in his room all alone.
He sits and dreams of planets when his parents are not home.
When Johnny gets older, he wants to go far away.
That's why he never feels like going out for the day.
He dreams about flying off to Mars

And dreams about seeing the moon and the sun and the stars.
He dreams about flying off to Mars
And dreams about seeing the moon and the sun and the stars.

The rings of Saturn are so cold.
When Johnny gets there he'll be a little too old.
The ice on Titan is far away.
But Johnny gets help from his friends called the Greys.

Hey hey Johnny hey hey. Why don't you ever want to come
    out and play?
Hey hey Johnny hey hey. Why don't you ever want to come
    out and play?

You see the aliens just go into Johnny's room.
They say they have a space base camp on the moon.
Johnny says they have big eyes and no hair.
He says they talk with their minds and like to stare.
Johnny just might find a faster way.
To travel through the dimensions on a spaceship made by the
    Greys.

Hey hey Johnny hey hey. Why don't you ever want to come
    out and play?
Hey hey Johnny hey hey. Why don't you ever want to come
    out and play?

Ann felt powerless to challenge Captain X, whom she saw as a
Nazi or vampire before her. Yet the Greys, as frightening an archetype as Nazis or vampires, offered her a weapon to compensate.
Much like any superhero archetype, space aliens possess superior
powers, so the Greys were the only force capable of challenging the
awesome power of the Nazis. It was as if the creative, intellectual
part of Ann's psyche was at war with some repressed subjugation

she felt deeply. Clashing violently inside her as well as in her projections on others, these forces battled for her allegiance.

Taking into consideration the absence of direct writing about emotions and her tendency to form an archetypal narrative, Ann's heavy use of symbol and metaphor made sense. And it is fascinating how all of her elements come together. In many ways, her desire to write science fiction and the prevalence of the alien Greys seem to provide her with an inner life that reflects the tension she refuses to admit in her own past.

If style is how the writer engages with her world, then we can see that Ann is a storyteller not yet in control of her own narrative. Like any effective storyteller, Ann must experience the raw emotions of her conflicts to achieve what Aristotle called catharsis. During her second visit to the military psychiatric ward, the alien Grey tells her, "A person can be mentally ill and intelligent at the same time." Yet Ann still struggles, some days accepting, some days denying that she is subject to manias. If stories offer us some lesson, Ann's story waits for her courage to internalize and express her mania as both burden and gift.

FIVE

"IN THE COAT CLOSET OF MY MIND"

Georgia

Some people say that one can tell what time of the day or night she was conceived by the time she was born. Usually if you are born in the night time, it is safe to say that conception was in the day. If this is true—and, as far as I know, no one has proven that theory wrong—I was conceived in the day in the month of January and nine months later on a Wednesday night I was born.

I was born at my home in Louisiana, delivered by a midwife as most people of that time were. Though both my parents were pleased to have me become a part of the family, I think in the beginning my father wished I had been born a male. But as time passed and he began to think straight, he was very pleased to have a female child. And his love for me was just as great as it would have been for a boy. Plus, I think that the old saying that a girl will always be loyal to her parents played a great part in the way many parents including mine felt about girl children. We could be depended on to keep the interest of the family as well as its secrets, hopes, and aspirations in mind, and we would teach these things to future generations. In other words, we were the keepers of what was important to our families. We were also the ones who would see to it that these things were taught to others just as our parents taught them to us.

My mother did not know when she bought me my first topcoat

since each topcoat would last about fifteen years or so. Mother told me that she bought the coat because the color and the price were right for her pocketbook. Plus she said, "Sister, I thought you, my darling, looked pretty spiffy in that beautiful blue double-breasted coat." Mother as well as others thought I looked just like a schoolteacher in my new coat. Well, maybe I did. But even if I did not, I was not going to argue with their wisdom. Whenever I was dressed up for whatever outing we would go on, I would do my "little girl strut." I was not sure that I wanted to share this coat with my sister though. Not because I wouldn't have been willing to share it with her had she treated her clothes a bit kinder, but to quote the adults of my childhood, "That child is just too hard on her clothes to suit me." But as fate would have it, not only did my sister, Miss Too Hard on Her Clothes, wear my coat but every child that followed her also wore that little blue coat that made me look like a schoolteacher. For a long time, I toyed with the idea of becoming a schoolteacher, but that's another story.

Maybe you could even say that my overcoat was a gender-changing coat because when Mother gave it to my eldest brother for his turn of wearing the blue wonder coat, she did not have to make buttonholes or remove buttons to ensure the maleness of the garment. The coat was made for either a boy or a girl with buttonholes on both sides so nothing had to be done to it when the boys' turn came to wear it. This coat was made child-worthy in every sense of the word. It was well built to last through even the most rough handling. It did get that type handling as time went by and wearers following me did not wear the coat as carefully as I did. For many years I was able to say just where my blue wonder coat had been retired but, with the passage of time, things get lost or replaced. And I guess that the coat has been misplaced once too many times. Or, maybe, horror of horrors, it is lost forever. Or maybe that is where it should be—in the coat closet of my mind. There it has been restored to its beauty. Oh, how wonderful it is to have rooms in your mind into which the most cherished memories can be enshrined in a museum just for such thoughts or remembrances.

MY MOM WOULD begin Christmas cooking early in the month of December. Why? Because she always made enough good-to-eat things to feed a small army. Not only did she bake a special cake for each family member but also a cook's special treat for herself. Altogether, this included seven cakes after my younger brother was born. But you might ask why she baked a cake for each child as well as for each adult? Well, there was a good reason for this, and that reason was that if our little friends came over, we could offer them cake without bothering the visiting family and adult company's cakes. Yes, Mother prepared other cakes for those who came by during Christmastime. All told, she often baked a total of sixteen cakes. None of them went to waste.

Mother always gave everyone in the family a sampling of a small, usually white-iced cake that was baked for Santa Claus to taste before he placed our presents in the special place by the fire hearth that was always set aside for gifts. Of course, I along with the other kids always had a sneaking feeling that our parents were really the people eating the cake and sipping the lemon-flavored tea. But, of course, we did not tell our parents what we thought. Just as long as they were happy in the thought that their kids would be happy with all of the bounty left in the special place by the fire by the night visitor—that was all that mattered. Never mind that we knew that they were Santa Claus. We had fun and our parents were pleased. You don't burst a bubble of hope, do you?

Except for one time that I wanted to burst my father's bubble. One Christmas my mother did not feel well and the buying of the Christmas toys fell to our father. Oh, how I wish you could have seen what he bought as toys for my sister and me. Those "space cadet" dolls were the ugliest toy dolls I had ever seen. Maybe they were the ugliest toys that had ever been invented up to that time. They had two painted ears on top of their heads plus two ears at the sides of their heads. There were several sets of eyes also, including the regular place on the front of their faces. Beside all of this, these dolls had just hideous screaming expressions on their faces. Instead of being for entertainment, I would say these toys were meant to throw scares into the hearts of youngsters who were supposed to be full of the devil. But my father thought that he could give these dolls to his two darlings. That Christmas was not on a par with other Christmases, and I hoped there would never be one of those sad, angry types again.

But back to the happening of other Christmas Eves at our house. One thing especially fascinated me about these Christmases of my childhood and that was the things that we youngsters helped Mother to do on Christmas Eve before we went to bed a little earlier than on other nights. One of these was the stuffing preparation. First, Mother made up several large skillets of cornbread which was cooked on top of the stove until done on both sides. Meanwhile, the other things for the stuffing were being made ready by each of us who were able to help, including Father. I would mince the livers and gizzards. If there were many of these, two persons would do it. Someone else, Sis perhaps, minced the meat from the neck of the bird. This would be added to the broth and onions, eggs, peppers, and seasonings that were added to the cooled and crumbled cornbread that had been cooked in the skillets earlier. Of course, the eggs were hard-boiled and minced. I do believe Mom used about four or six eggs for her stuffing. Not only did we use the liquid that the giblets had been cooked in, but we also used some of the liquid from the pot in which the bird had been parboiled. Yes, even as I write these lines, I can taste that cornbread mixture, and the aroma comes back so real that if I didn't know better, I would reach out on the desk and try some stuffing. Yes, we enjoyed being Momma's expert tasters. Expert because we hadn't adulterated our tasters yet. And Daddy always knew just what taste Mom was looking for also. He had educated his taste buds to remember a special taste and that stuffing didn't go into the bird until it was melting-in-your-mouth ready.

I cannot describe the incredibly delicious and satisfying aroma that came from our oven when Mom would put the stuffing-filled bird inside the oven to be cooked until well done, still moist and not dry. Since the turkey didn't require constant watching, we could then help Mom to clean and put away whatever cooking utensils that needed to be cleaned. Then we scrubbed the floor. We set Santa's plate covered with a napkin on the table. Then we were off to bed. Mother went to bed at that time also. But she would get up later and baste the bird if it needed basting. Some homegrown birds didn't need too much basting because my mother would place pats of specially prepared basting butter mixtures in strategic places on the bird's body. Plus, by using the old-fashioned roaster with the knobby dome lid, the only thing needed was to close the lid and let the bird cook slowly until done. Why is this, you ask? The moisture that collected on the dome of the knobby lid would condense and drip onto the food, keeping it fork-tender and melting-in-your-mouth delicious.

Usually sometime during Christmas Eve before we turned in for the night, we always got around to reading the Christmas story from the Bible plus other stories related to Christmas from other books. We would sing carols and pray also. This was always done before the last-minute baking and cooking was completed because even the baby was required to be at the worship time. Don't get me wrong. Prayer and worship time were practiced in our home throughout the year, but at Christmas we always had a special little program with carols and hymn-singing, reciting Bible verse or poetry. Every year we would repeat that famous Christmas poem "The Night Before Christmas." I believe Mother loved this poem just as much as we did because it was the first long poem she recited in a school Christmas pageant that according to Mother was a big thing at her school, heralding vacation time as well as Christmas-time for both staff and pupils.

Chocolate icing-making was another family affair in our house. I began the icing process, and my father would cut into very small slivers the several chocolate blocks that Mother bought to make the frosting with. These slivers of chocolate went into the top half of a double boiler to melt slowly over hot water. To the melted chocolate, Mother added butter and powdered XX sugar, which she mixed well adding a bit of milk if it was needed to keep the frosting mixture at a just right spreading consistency. The first step of preparing the cake icing is the addition of the flavoring agent, whether it was vanilla or some other flavoring agent. This is added after the mixture has cooled so that the taste will be true. The big moment comes when the gooey velvety brown stuff was spread on the outside and top of each layer of the chocolate cakes. Mother made at least two of these decadent works of edible art. You may be beginning to think that we didn't eat any ordinary foods at Christmastime. Well, let me tell you, it wasn't just sweets and treats. Mother saw to it that biscuits and cornbread were baked and stored properly to be eaten during the serving of holiday fare.

I can remember waking up one Christmas day at about 10:30 in the morning. We had already been up much earlier to check out toys and go get apples, nuts, and hot tea with cake at Grandpa's house. If some things that we enjoy doing over and over are the beginnings of family tradition, you could say that our early Christmas morning visit to the home of our elders was a tradition in our family. As far back as I can remember and as long as my grandpa lived close by, we made it our business to visit him first thing on Christmas mornings. In the beginning, we had to wait until it was light outside because of our small size. Although our houses were not that far apart, we obeyed our mother's wishes to wait until the sun had come up. When my sister and I got bigger, we began going to Grandpa's house a bit earlier than when we were tots. During our childhood, one could walk around even in the early light of dawn unafraid most of the time. Don't get me wrong. I am not trying to say that our neck of the woods was a utopian place. Neither would I say that it was an ideal place, completely free of danger. We lived in a real world where things happened, and sometimes these things weren't good. But praises be to God, my siblings and I made it through those early years despite the tempo of those days. Maybe traveling in groups with good riding crops and a pair of dogs trained to take care of us helped also.

But back to Christmases. After we would return home, my sisters, brothers, and I would go back to bed for a snooze before breakfast. Mother and Daddy would get up shortly after we returned from Grandpa's place, build a fire in the stove so that the kitchen would warm up, and make a breakfast fit for a king. We had hot buttered biscuits (jam was available if someone needed it), scrambled eggs with bacon bits (just enough to give the eggs a festive appearance), grits, and oily sausages that Mother had done in a cream sauce after slicing the sausages into one-inch rounds and sealing the juices by browning the pieces in a bit of oil. We had hot lemon tea or we could have milk if we wanted it. Yes, you could say we didn't go completely crazy not even at Christmastime. We knew that good nutrition meant a lot. It is all right to enjoy the feast of holiday dining, but don't forget that even too much of a good thing can be too much. Part of our Christmas menu always read like this: greens, potato salad, fresh vegetable salad, cornbread muffins or biscuits, corn, and green peas. Indeed there was bounty at our table because we had great success with growing vegetables.

Of course, we hung pretty curtains and set beautifully appointed tables and saw to it that every nook and cranny of the house as well as the yard was shipshape for the holidays. Yes, we kept a well-manicured lawn, and since the weather is generally mild where I grew up, we could eat on our porch or in the yard if we so chose. I still think that a snowless Christmas day is wonderful and truly a blessing because that is the way I remember the weather being at this time of year in my hometown. As a matter of fact, most of the year the weather was balmy and comfortable. Oh, there was winter coldness and stormy seasons, but overall our weather was the best there was outside of the islands in the north Atlantic Ocean.

SHE WASN'T OUR real grandmother, but she was married to our grandpa. And in those days when I grew up, one was expected to give respect where it was due. In this case, to call this large evil-looking woman "Grandma" was doing just that.

I know that all of us have had things that frighten us. And one thing that frightened my sister when she was a small child was the lowly chicken feather. Why she would run from another child if he or she had a feather in hand I haven't figured out to this day, but she was afraid of a chicken feather for most of her childhood. Grandma was afraid of thunderstorms. She always thought that people were trying to do her harm by voodoo magic. She wouldn't live in a house for long if she couldn't "ghost- and voodoo-proof" it. Nailing up horseshoes over the outer entrances to the house was supposed to do the trick. The way to do this was to nail horseshoes with the open ends pointing upward over the entrances of our houses. Because if this was done, then the metal from the horseshoe set up a special field around the doors which kept evil and unwanted spirits out of the house. And this kept those inside or those who lived there safe.

It was also my granny who said that, if you wore a dime tied around the ankle with a string, you would be able to tell whether or not someone had "throwed" at you. In other words, you would be able to tell if someone had conjured on you. According to Granny, "if the dimes remained silver in color, all was well, but if one or both of the dimes turned black or some other off-color, you had been hoo-dooed or roots had been worked on you." The stronger the root work, the more the dimes would change color. Plus she thought that wearing dimes around the ankles would help keep evil things from entering the body if one happened to step on them. She also believed that an ax blade could be waved at an approaching storm cloud and the cloud would rise above your home. Of course, you had to read some Bible verses before you waved the ax at the clouds. We did not think much of her old sayings, but she did not seem to mind. At every chance, she would mention something about the stuff she had been taught to believe by her mother when she was growing up in Westlake.

I suppose that everyone has a family member who claims to have a special brand of sayings that should be passed on to the next generation. In this way, a family history becomes a way to preserve and protect the future of the family. Well, I guess you could say that my grandma was of this notion because she certainly had some old wives' tales that she thought fit into this legacy.

One of these bits of wisdom dealt with how to prevent unwanted company from visiting your house. And this is what she said: "When the person is just about ready to leave your house, go into the kitchen and get some table salt, and put it in a cloth or something you can get to easily. Don't let the person see you do this." Now once you had the salt packed away secretly in the cloth, you were to place the bundle in the back of your dress. When the visitor got up to leave, you had to follow him or her to the gate or wherever your yard ended, and sprinkle salt behind the person as you walked behind him out of the yard. She said, "While doing this, you must not let the visitor become aware of what you are doing because the salt sprinkling wouldn't work."

Grandma also thought that if you stubbed your toe on a rock or something, it was bad luck. To prevent this bad luck, you had to turn around three times before continuing on your way. If a person stubbed his toe when he was approaching another person's doorstep, front entrance, or even the yard, this meant that he was not welcome at that place. I often wondered what it meant in the case when you stubbed your toe before entering your own house. After all, one is supposed to be welcome at one's own home. At least, that's the way I see it. Of course, I did not ask her to explain that to me because I did not want to embarrass or anger her. If she couldn't see the folly in her toe-stubbing words of wisdom, I wasn't going to burst her bubble.

The last bit of wisdom I heard often in our house when Granny came for a visit was the black cat myth. According to the myth, if a person was traveling on a road and a black cat went across from the right side to the left side of the road, then the person not only had to stop and turn around in a circle three times but whirl around in a circle three times. If this was not done, bad luck was sure to follow soon.

Well, I guess the above examples are enough evidence to let you know that my stepgrandma's wisdom was neither conventional nor did it have rhyme or reason except that which the old woman gave to it. Some people would say that her wisdom was only the cluckings of an old hen. Maybe that is true or maybe one had to believe in order for this wisdom to work. To make a judgment call at this date would not validate or invalidate it. Or maybe, like my mother told me about the "wise one," we should just let her spout her sayings. After all, we knew that many of these sayings were just old tales that Granny thought were helpful. Mother told us, "You have been given the best words of wisdom there is, and that, my daughter, is the word of God. So use your head!" And that is just what I did. You know, dear reader, I am very glad that I did use my head. So, I say to you, dear friends, just read the words because these words are part of a great whole and it really doesn't seem to matter if they make sense.

EVERY FAMILY IN the South and in my community had its own set of idiosyncrasies. Some of our idiosyncrasies were names we used for things. We called a sofa a "do-be-four." A "spider" was a large three-legged chicken fryer or a ranch skillet. High-top shoes were called "brogans." The outhouse was and in some parts of the Deep South still is the "outside toilet," or as my granny used to call it the "doodie closet." Then there were the "smokehouses," which were not houses at all but were large sheds in the backyard of every farmer. The tool shed was not the same as the meat- or smokehouse. This smokehouse was equipped with a place in the center where a special smoking rock was set up so that the meat hanging from the rafters could be cured properly. Hickory chips and other nice-smelling wood chips were placed on the smoking rock until the meat was cured.

Before the days of the vegetable crisper that is inside the bottom of the refrigerator, we had a "potato bunk": a hole in the ground was set up to keep vegetables and some hardy fruits during the bad or cold times of the year. Instead of relaxing on the porch, we relaxed on the "garry." Then there were the "loggers' coat" and the "mackinaw," both of which men wore in the wintertime. When a woman canned food in my hometown, she was said to be "putting up food."

LIVING ON A farm had its ups and its downs. As I sit here thinking about when I was a little girl growing up down south, one thing in particular comes to mind. And that is the time my father bought my sister and me a pair of boy's brogan shoes. Believe me when I tell you those were the only shoes that would not tear up. No matter how hard I would try to tear those "brogs" up, they seemed to get stronger and stronger. I really don't know why my father bought us those awful shoes because to this day no one has ever told us why. Sometimes I believe that my father would have been happier had all of his children been boys. But then, that's another story.

Some things are remembered because of unpleasantness. For other things, they are remembered for the pleasure they bring. The uniquely squeaky clean smell and feel of starched curtains, table-cloths, and other clean house smells not only at holiday time but throughout the year will always be with me. I think that because we lived out in the country, one could almost smell the health-giving rays of the sun. There's a saying that people should air out their city houses at least during the spring and fall seasons. I wonder why these seasons and not the others. Maybe the milder of the four sea-sons were picked because of the sweetness that is in the air when the buds begin to open and the softness of the breeze as time moves toward coldness once again. Anyway, whatever the reasons for air-ing out one's home could never apply to homes in the country because due to the way country houses are constructed, there is no need for special time of airing out because cross-ventilation is always in play. And that does give a home a plus, so far as smelling fresh is concerned. Our homes were little havens of freshness and pure clean air.

Fresh flowers and plants were not only a part of the landscape but also a part of the decorating scheme. Not all of the plants were nurs-ery stock. Many of them grew wild. But all in all, I can say that we never lacked in the art of having plants, foliage or flowering, around us gracing our tables as centerpieces or being used in other places such as wall niches in decorative pots or vases. Plus my father knew how to make ornaments from young pliable twigs and other green plants. And we had many wonderful wreaths and other flower/ foliage arrangements throughout the year. Being in an area of the United States where the weather is mild almost year round, we were blessed to have access to many different types of live plants that Father tended and culled with care all the time. Truly I could say that our yard was a master work of art thanks to Nature (God) and to Daddy who used his knowledge of what plants needed to turn them into a work of art and beauty. You could say that we were very blessed in many ways. And much of these blessings rubbed off on each of us kids. We in turn use this to help make the world around us a little more beautiful, whether it is through serving good food or making our homes works of art through decoration, hard work, and much prayer.

I remember life on the farm, especially after I grew big enough to take on responsibility such as being able to cook in the kitchen alone. I made extra pocket money through my cake baking. Sometimes I would sell at least three cakes by the slice along with the several whole cakes that some people ordered. When I was a child, my grandfather said that he would not eat any food that a child had prepared. But lo and behold, he changed his tune on the day I made my first batch of cornmeal pancakes.

It was a rainy morning and the folks, my grandparents, came to visit us early. So early, in fact, that we had not had any breakfast yet. My mother said to me, "Well, Sister, today I am going to allow you to prepare and cook the pancakes." I squalled a big yippee because I was so glad to be in charge of breakfast fixin's. So I set out getting everything ready and mixed. Just about that time in walked my grandparents. After everyone finished with the pleasantries, my mom and I set the table, and I began serving up hotcakes to order. My parents did not give away the secret of who had prepared breakfast, not even when my grandfather said, "These are really delicious battercakes." I think my parents wanted to build up a good deal of enthusiasm about the fine quality of my battercakes before announcing that they had been prepared by me, one of the persons whose food Granddad had said he would not eat. And he had, of everyone at breakfast that morning, consumed about six large pancakes. And he alone was ranting joyfully about those being the size he most enjoyed eating rather than those quarter-sized cakes most people pawned off as pancakes. Yes, the man was sold. I knew that, if I had won him over with my first meal, the future in that area was rosy. It was about an hour or so before finally one of my parents casually said, "Listen, we have got an announcement to make. But first off, Dad, what do you think made breakfast so wonderful and then we'll tell you our great revelation."

I do believe my grandpa was a little taken aback. His entire face was a question mark. As if to say, pancakes are pancakes. Looking at him, you could tell that he was a bit puzzled. Plus he could hardly wait for one of my parents to give the big revelation. So after hedging for awhile, and going around the bush, Father decided that he would tell him who was responsible for preparing such a good morning repast. To begin, my father said, "Daddy, do you remember when you told us that you would not eat a child's cooking?" With a grin on his face, my grandpa replied, "Yes, I do." My father was enjoying this, and with a twinkle in his eye, he continued the questioning: "And do you also remember that other statement that you made at the time in question?" By now, my grandfather was beginning to suspect that he had put his foot in his mouth, and before he answered the second question, he said, "I am beginning to feel as though I will soon be eating my words. Is this true?" For several minutes, neither man said a word. You could almost feel the anticipation, the air was so thick. I think that Dad was enjoying himself very much.

Finally he was tired of seeing Grandpa squirm, so he said, "Well, Daddy, I think it is time for you to eat some crow because Sister is the person to whom accolades are due because it is she who is responsible for serving such a great and delicious meal. Do you still believe that a child can't cook well enough to please you?" But this wasn't enough for Daddy because he hammered on, "Are you now ready to admit my baby has got the makings of becoming a great cook one of these days? And are you now ready to admit that you were wrong in saying that children don't know how to do adult jobs?"

Then the old gentleman called me over to him and put his arms around my shoulder. He proceeded to apologize to me personally. I was thrilled and pleased because now I knew that my grandpa really did believe in me and my ability to prepare appetizing meals.

WHEN I WAS growing up, adult women and the female children would have quilting parties. Maybe we didn't have a lot of quilting parties, but we did do a great deal of quilting. Yes, there were always enough quilts to keep everyone warm and also some leftovers in case overnight company came by. Many of the quilts that we made were what you might call fancy piecework and others weren't so fancy. One pattern that I particularly liked was called the Pig's Pen. This quilt was made by sewing thin strips around the four sides of a square until the block was about twelve inches square. Once the total number of these pig pens were made, four triangular shaped pieces were sewn to each block. Then, straight strips joined the squares together until there were five in a row and the rows were in turn joined by long four foot wide strips until the quilt top was completed. Then, this top along with the cotton batting was placed in stretching frames and quilted in fancy designs until the quilt was finished. Finally, the finished quilt was hemmed on all sides and was ready for winter use.

Around my house, washday was on Monday. The day started early partly because much of the washing was done by hand and also because most people wanted to be done with this chore to get some rest before beginning the cooking for supper. The washing of clothes followed an age-old ritual of boiling, bleaching, and bluing. Now, if I don't relate this as some of you readers may remember, try not to say I am wrong because, although it may not follow your procedure, this was our way. We boiled white things in water mixed with soap shavings. Then, with a special stick, we removed the hot clothes from the pan of hot water. The pan, by the way, was really a large, three-legged pot heated over an open fire in the summer months, and in the winter, it was heated in the kitchen. Still dripping wet, the clothes were placed into a tub of room-temperature water and then rubbed on a rubboard or scrubboard for a few minutes. After the scrubbing, we placed the clothes in the first rinse mixture of bleach and water. After wringing the clothes out, they were rinsed again in water to which bluing sticks had been added. Bluing helps to release any bleach and soap residue that may still be in the fibers. With this done, the whites including light colors and bed linens were hung on the line to dry. Then, the whole process was repeated again, minus the bleach, for the colored clothes. Yes, we used a great deal of water on washday.

Washday at my house was a family affair because everyone old enough to help with the several sequences of this chore did something, from keeping the fire hot enough to ensuring the bluing mixture was the correct temperature. Not only that, but these clothes and linens had to be folded and put away. Those that needed ironing were put into the pressing basket until the next day. Yes, Tuesday was ironing day at my house, especially during the summer months when school wasn't in session. During the school year, we ironed our school clothes on Saturday night. We had to prepare enough clothes to last at least a week because we weren't allowed to use the flat irons or the electric iron just when we wanted. My mother always said, "Everything must be done at a certain time. Ya'll have to learn to use your time wisely." I can understand now why she gave us that advice. It has helped us to keep and set priorities and work within a given time frame when time is of the essence.

Now ironing day, as I recall, wasn't as big of a deal as the day before. The most important reminder was that until our brothers became old enough to help with the ironing, the chore fell on my sister and me. For this reason, each of us was responsible for her own clothes as well as one brother. Some of our better clothes were done by either Mother or by the local cleaners. Everything else including linens was done by the family. On occasion, I would trade chores with my middle brother. He did my ironing, and I would do something he had to do. I did this because each of us could iron well enough to please our mother. I believe that my middle brother is by far the best ironer of all of us. All and all, I guess you could say that at least our clothes were clean and neat. And yes, they were well fitting also.

One of the things that I remember about my childhood is the Saturday night suppers that Mother would serve to us on the side lawn. Once everything had been cooked, she would serve the food to each of us as though we were in a restaurant. That was great fun. And all of us learned how one should act under different circumstances. Not only did we have fun, we learned how to set the table, bus the dishes, and do whatever else one needs to do in order to make a cafe clean and ready for the next person.

WHEN I FIRST met Mrs. Thomas, our schoolteacher, I could not believe that she was an adult because she was just a wee bit taller than I was at age five. I guess what tipped me off was that she was rounded or fatter than any kid I knew. She had a large head and acres of thick once-black hair which she wore with a part in the middle and two long plaits that either hung down or were pinned up atop her head with hair bows. Sometimes these braids were done in what is called the French way. And when she wanted to look dressy, she would pile it high in a beehive. One would have probably said that she wasn't a fashionable dresser, but to me, she wore the things that were appropriate for the type of work she did with us youngins.

When she opened her mouth and began to talk to us, we were reassured without a doubt that this round short person was truly a grownup. Not only that, but she was fully capable of handling a room of small fries like myself. We knew from day one that this lady who had to stand on a box to reach the top of the blackboard wasn't going to stand for a lot of nonsense. If to teach means to mold a mind and help it grow and blossom into a thinking machine, everyone's parent knew that this round person was the one for the job.

Before I tell you about her impact on my life, let me tell you some things about her. For one thing, though she and her husband never had children of their own, they adopted two children of a family who lived in their neighborhood. They raised these children to adulthood. In my mind, one had to be both loving and generous as well as a patient soul to want to deal with children on a full-time basis in the capacity of a mommy, even when she didn't have to do so. But that is just what she and her husband decided to do. Not only that, but they also helped another family keep their daughter in school by contributing warm clothes and money when it was needed. I often wondered how she could do this on a teacher's salary, but I eventually found out that besides her teaching career, she and Mr. Thomas had a well-established and thriving business. It was rare to have any type of business in our neck of the woods because, for the most part, this was all farming country. And one would think that this would be the business of choice, but the Thomases went against the odds and invested their money in a tailoring business, not knowing if it would fly or not. But fly it did, growing from just adjusting hemlines of Mrs. Thomas's friends to a thriving tailoring business that flourished for many years, even after Mrs. Thomas retired from teaching. Maybe they paid their tithes and God did what He said He would do, "fill up their coffers full to running over." I never talked to Mrs. Thomas about this, but since she was a churchgoing woman, perhaps that was true of their blessings.

Anyway, I can say that our classroom was voted the best of the parish of Red River. This included the creature comforts from carts for snoozing to the friezes that decorated the top of our classroom. I guess those long brown paper drawings that bordered the bottom of the room were called friezes also. And not only did this lady know how to teach little ones the tools it would take to make it through the rest of their school years, but she knew how to train one in the art of bodybuilding. To do that she had to get down in the sandbox with us. No, she did not turn into a kid herself; she was still in charge. But that lady had us doing all sorts of things that would help us to develop our muscles and gain the strength that one needs as one gets bigger. Well, I guess you can see from what I have said that this woman was sort of like the old country doctor, a general practitioner, because she could do all the things that every elementary teacher has to do today. And she did them very well, I might add.

Before I went to school, I was able to count to a hundred. I could write several of the times table groups from start to finish. And I knew the alphabet and could read things such as writing on matchboxes, cereal boxes, and road signs. When I did enter school, I thought that this was one of the best things that could have happened to me. I had finally gotten to that little place of learning known as the schoolhouse. I knew right from the start that my folks would expect me, maybe demand from me, that I do my best work, even in the lower grades. So right away I said to myself I had better do what my parents wanted me to do.

Mrs. Thomas didn't just teach us the alphabet and numbers but laid the foundation for what would help us to be the best people we could be, not only while we were still in school but, as I found out, years later. Some of the things Mrs. Thomas said were words of wisdom anyone could use at anytime in a life. When she was talking to us about the importance of being neat and clean, no matter how many or how few clothes a person has, she would say that kids should learn how to wash and press their own clothes at a very early age. By the time they had become teenagers or were ready for the responsibility, whichever came first, the child would already have made taking care of his or her clothes second nature and when you left home for college or marriage, laundry day would not be drudgery day.

I often thought Mrs. Thomas and my mother secretly met and exchanged ideas. Their words of wisdom were the same: it was never too early to teach people how to take good care of themselves. Because in reality that is what adults are doing when they teach us things such as how to make sure your shoes are tied and your face is clean before you leave for school or work in the mornings.

I guess for the most part we are glad to have had such people in our lives when we were growing up.

DISCUSSION

Deborah Pugh

Hands and hearts of people who have grown up in the country never forget their connections to the land. In the work of southern writers, the land prevails—whether in the longing for it or the urge to move beyond it. For Georgia and all those who have left the land of their youth for cities, these two desires clash, as the urban transplant struggles with the piercing words of Proust, "the true paradises are paradises we have lost."

I met Georgia on a cold winter morning at Rachael's House, the drop-in day shelter for homeless women in Washington, D.C., where I was conducting a class in oral storytelling. Five students and I were huddled around my old cassette player in front of the triple bay windows when Georgia walked in the front door and observed the group. Near the end of class, I summarized oral storytelling and paved the way for our next writing challenge: autobiography. I don't know how long Georgia had been observing me or previous classes, but when she sat down and started talking, my intuition told me something wonderful was in the making.

However, first I had to pass Georgia's muster. She would not offer her most precious possession—her memoirs—to me if she thought I would try to censor what she called her old country words or her conversational style of writing. Most of all, she would not risk working with me if she thought I would see her as just another homeless woman and not as an individual. Clutching the handles of her stuffed black-vinyl book bag, Georgia eased out her questions in a rural southern accent that sang to my heart. Yet there was no doubt in my mind that this was a test to gauge sincerity, to root out phoniness, and most of all, to ensure that her integrity would be respected.

To varying degrees, all of us give this test to others; however, for Georgia, the results were critical in deciding whom she shut out and whom she accepted into her life. Her standards were firmly in place, but these boundaries had less to do with rigid judgments than with her strong sense of identity as a nonconforming individualist. Although she had been living in Washington since 1969, something "down home" lived deep in Georgia; she would not forsake it for acceptance in the status-conscious urban world. For this, I believe she paid a heavy price as most nonconformists do, particularly in terms of job opportunities; but, as she told me once, "I'm just who I am, and that's good enough."

Born in a town called Section 16 in the mid-1940s, Georgia's family moved in her first year to the Red River Parish of Louisiana. In those lowland plains, rich alluvial soil is deposited on previous generations of earth by lakes and the Red River. Corn, beans, and cotton grow there on small scratched-out patches as well as on old plantations. After slavery, the sharecropping system that grew up in its place became both the means of livelihood and the plight of many black people, including Georgia's father. He was more fortunate than other sharecroppers, Georgia says, because he was given his own small plot on which to grow food for their family. Others were not so lucky.

After Georgia finished high school in the mid-1960s, she entered Grambling College in Grambling, Louisiana, where she stayed for almost a year. What happened at Grambling was indicative of Georgia's struggle against the limited roles her family and society offered her. First, a professor wanted Georgia to come to her house as a live-in housekeeper and cook. This position did not pay, but the professor assured Georgia she could "fix" her grades in exchange.

Next, although the context is not clear, Georgia's mother argued with the professor and withdrew Georgia (who had wanted to earn her grades) from the college. Part of the reason apparently was that her father needed an operation, and the family decided that Georgia's tuition money should go for that purpose. Also around this time, Georgia wanted to join the military, but her father forbade it, so she and her sister decided to move to Washington. When promised jobs there did not materialize, the sisters took keypunch classes at Washington Technical Institute. During that time, Georgia also worked at Fort McNair as a clerk/secretary until it closed down.

For over a decade, Georgia, her sister, and her sister's son lived together in an apartment, but after a visit from a welfare worker, Georgia's sister began to fear that she would lose her assistance because the apartment did not have enough rooms for its occupants. For this reason, in 1982 Georgia packed her belongings and headed for a homeless shelter until she could get back on her feet. In 1985, she left the shelter to take a job as a live-in nursing assistant for a woman in Maryland; but by 1987, the job ended, and Georgia returned to her sister's apartment, surviving on a series of temporary jobs as a nursing companion. In 1990, she applied and was admitted to Strayer College in the Washington area where she is now one year away from graduating with a bachelor's degree in business. She is still living in her sister's apartment.

To describe Georgia beyond these events of her life is not simple, for she is something of a riddle: her inner story, guarded by an extreme sense of privacy, gives way only to her outer story of hopes and dreams, and leaves angers and fears hidden deep within her. As a result, Georgia appears to be a woman of incredible fortitude whom people feel they will never really know. Although she and I are close friends, even I have come to believe that there are places in Georgia's life to which no one will ever have access. Whenever I gave autobiographical writing exercises at Rachael's, for instance, I tried to balance assignments between happy and sad moments in life. Yet Georgia would never write about hard memories, always opting instead for those memories that were pleasurable and empowering. In class one day, the women were reading their assignments out loud. It was very difficult listening to one painful memory after another; the tragedies were overwhelming. When Georgia's turn came, she first said she couldn't think of anything to write, but then she let a little piece of herself come through. She told how she had once wanted to join the military for the adventure, travel, and education, but her father had not allowed it. As she spoke, just for one instant, her whole persona changed. The terrible disappointment elongated her face; her words were punctuated with sighs; her eyes filled with tears that she did not let fall.

Of course, there are as many explanations for why people shy away from bad memories as there are people. My own grandmother—a very strong woman—would do the same, making comments like "you can't live yesterday today so what's the use studying about it." I felt both my grandmother and Georgia had placed their bad memories on the back shelf for safety, either because they did not want to appear weak or because they could not bear to relive their tragedies. A third alternative, especially for women, is the fact that narrative space closes up because of powerful influences that have silenced them. At Grambling, whether the professor's offer was generous or exploitative, Georgia leaves much unsaid, but it must have been a time of tremendous pain for her. As for most women, loyalty to family clashes frequently with individual goals and identity, and this dilemma is often covered up with silence. While Georgia says her family's removing her from college and refusing to let her join the military left her with no choice, the aching to be more than what others thought she could be lives in her to this day.

IN EVERY STORY we tell and particularly in autobiography, the structure and content are directed by both our own attempts to make sense of our lives and the requirements of the storytelling moment. Even in the stories we tell each other in the normal course of a day, our selection of details and the way we present them are dictated by our audience and our purpose. In the process of writing her memoirs, Georgia allowed herself to catch memories as they came. She began each segment with "I Remember _____" and then filled in the blank with topics such as Christmas, Grandma, Me-Georgia, When I fixed pancakes for Grandpa, Washday, etc. Georgia's decision to approach her autobiography in this way helps explain what she hoped to achieve and why.

Clearly, Georgia has taken the role of family historian. It is an important role; however, it is one that takes precedence over Georgia's own identity and aspirations. She says, "we [the girl children] could be depended on to keep the interest of the family as well as its secrets, hopes, and aspirations in mind." This is a tremendous burden on a woman who imagines a different life for herself, and it is particularly debilitating when the time comes to make narrative decisions in autobiography: Whom do I place at the center of the story—myself or the family legacy? Do I write about myself as I actually was or how I was expected to be?

Examining Georgia's perspectives as protagonist (the lead character) and narrator (the teller of the story) of her writing offers some clues as to the design of her narrative. Georgia as narrator provides the controlling intelligence that guides the story. With a couple of exceptions, we do not see her as protagonist, acting and interacting with other characters in such a way as to product plot; rather, she has forced herself to limit her narrative to the interest of the family. I found it interesting that if I pushed Georgia in our discussions, she would admit her anger over her family's decisions restricting her career options. However, no references to those events or her feelings about them appear in her writing. Perhaps this is because her memoirs are not complete; the autobiographical process is still in the beginning stages.

Of course, if Georgia's goal is to pass on to her niece and nephew some idea of what used to be, then she does achieve that. Most of the memories she chooses to write about fit into what is called "transmissive memory." Transmissive remembering allows the storyteller to pass on a legacy or heritage and to explain values of a bygone era. Georgia recounts precise details of cooking, washing, quilting, and Christmas traditions. Although these memories are folkloric and a glimpse into material culture, what cannot be overlooked is that her audience for this writing was not only her niece and nephew, but also herself—for what she has written is what she yearns to read. Like most people at middle age, Georgia looks back more and more on the past and wants to transmit a legacy. Some people may try to locate examples of past accomplishments and understand how those achievements have led to their present satisfactions. Others may see such a stark contrast between the past and the present that those previous times offer a way either to heal or to escape current pain. For Georgia, perhaps both are true. She began work on this project shortly after her experience with homelessness and during the time that she is a college student. For her, the state of uncertainty and powerlessness inherent in homelessness is giving way to the accomplishment of attending college; as the power to control her life returns, the writing of memoirs begins.

Although many of the memories Georgia writes about are meant to explain family values, an undercurrent to her reminiscences reflects her present-day concerns and suggests that her dominant motive in life is the quest for self-sufficiency. Above all else, what Georgia dreams of today is a home of her own and employment; she equates these accomplishments with respect and independence. But although she dreams of her future, somewhere deep inside she may doubt that she can attain her goals. For this reason, she shapes her memoirs as an untroubled time of family strength to serve as a balm to soothe her present concerns.

Anyone who has farmed for a living, especially as a sharecropper, knows the hard work, harsh circumstances, and ever-present uncertainties of that life. Yet in Georgia's memoirs we do not see specific instances of struggling against adversity. In fact, there is little adversity at all except a brief mention of a Christmas when her father brought home dolls that his daughters thought were ugly. Most of her memories are idyllic, centered in childhood's simpler times, and focused on family cooperation and self-sufficiency. Because of this and Georgia's reluctance to write about bad times, it would seem that her reminiscences also act as a means of coping: "how wonderful it is," she writes, "to have rooms in your mind into which the most cherished memories can be enshrined in a museum just for . . . thoughts or remembrances."

For this particular time in Georgia's life, her mental museum provides her with a quiet, majestic refuge from the hard facts of city life. There is no spot for a garden in the apartment complex where she lives still with her sister and nephew. Food comes from the store when she has the money. If there is no money, she eats at the lunch and dinner programs at shelters. Her front lawn is bare clay, tramped down and littered with bottles, cans, and candy wrappers. Crack dealers hang out in the court in front of her apartment and hide their goods in apartments abandoned years ago. When gunfire pops like Fourth of July fireworks, she keeps her eyes glued to the sidewalk, to the sky, or anywhere other than in the direction of the young warlords on the corner. And she waits, like in the early morning hours when the police barricaded her apartment complex to arrest drug dealers and confiscate illegal weapons. She waits until her time has come to leave, and until then, she goes to the museum in her mind to fortify her belief that leaving is possible.

The very aspects of life that are absent or muted in her present situation loom large in her memoir. How Georgia shaped her writing and why she chose particular memories to write about came partly from her experience with homelessness. During our time together, Georgia wrote and talked a good bit about being homeless. The following is from one of her writings:

Shelter Life

Just what is meant by shelter life? What is life like with the confines of the overnight shelter or temporary lodging place for those who have been displaced by society's rules or for some other reason? Some may prefer the often-used phrase "fallen through the cracks." I would use the word "displaced." Whatever word or phrase that one wants to use makes no sense unless one has been there. Yes, you would know what displacement means in a general sense but to apply this "falling through the cracks" to a whole generation of people is almost unbelievable even to those who have lived this nightmare. What cracks, you may ask. These cracks, these fissures allowed to become so wide until a great ditch came into being and all these people fell through. Think about it. There would have to be a mighty force behind any group of people to cause so many of them to fall through these cracks.

Since the phrase is not, never was, and never will be the correct one to apply to the homeless situation, I will use the terms "displaced" or "displacement." There were many reasons that people became displaced in the decade of the early 1980s. Some of these were: absent husbands, death of a spouse, loss of income, inability to work and baby-sit a small child at the same time, sickness, disability due to illness, evictions because of unemployment, insufficient wages to cover all the necessary expenses. So you starved or you froze. Terrible choices in this land of plenty.

Though I haven't elaborated upon the above reasons, I do believe they will give you an idea as to what I am talking about. Oh, I am not going to tell what you may want to hear. I am going to tell you the truth as it was when I was there in that bizarre system called homelessness. According to an article the press wrote when I was homeless, homelessness was brought about by a group of people who were lazy, drunkards, or mentally ill persons. They were folks who were looking for handouts and for someone to take care of them. Basically, those statements were bogus and unfounded in truth.

Many of the people who set up the rules and regulations for those who would run shelters never gave it a thought as to how long it would take a person to get back on their feet after he or she had become displaced. Instead they put a ceiling on things and that was three-five months minimum and five-nine months maximum. And in the case of the loss of a loved one through death or divorce, it takes upwards to six months for the initial hurt to ease up. And it is at this time that a person doesn't need to be rushed through any system. Did the big-wigs ask any questions of non-displaced people to see how long it would take a normal (yes, people are normal even in a displaced capacity) human being to recover from such things as a bad divorce? They did not want to deal with the people on this basis. They wanted to deal with them in a degrading and inhumane way. So instead of trying to be realistic, they decided to set up what for many people was a set of rules that proved to be impossible.

Therefore, instead of helping these people to become main-stream again, they helped them to become depressed and thus unable to cope with life as one should cope. Many people become temporarily mentally unbalanced, because they were not that way from the start. So you could say that it was this system of shelter life that caused many people to become ill. Because they did not give them time to recover from what had brought them to this state of affairs. Now don't get me wrong, some people like that were on the street at the time I am writing about, but this segment of displaced people in no way made up the bulk of the people who used temporary lodging in the early '80s.

It is not ironic at all, but perfectly logical, that a person who feels so violated in the circumstances of homelessness would begin to write about her past home. Her experience with being pigeonholed in homelessness and with the anonymity of the city impinges on her sense of self in such a way that remembering times when she felt powerful and capable helps her establish the link between then and now. The memory of preparing pancakes for her grandfather speaks to successful performance and surprising people with her capabili-ties. In her little blue wonder coat, not only did she feel so beauti-ful she would do the "little girl strut," but everyone told her she looked like a schoolteacher. Immediately after this episode, she says,

"For a long time, I toyed with the idea of becoming a schoolteacher, but that's another story." It is a story untold because of painful memories, missed opportunities, or twists of fate; yet it may be a story that is unfolding in Georgia's present role as college student. Being told she looked like a schoolteacher and being prized for both attractiveness and intelligence provide Georgia with her earliest images of herself.

Not too surprisingly, we also find these qualities in her early role model, the schoolteacher Mrs. Thomas. Although Mrs. Thomas is not imposing physically, she rules her elementary school with a compassionate, loving, but disciplined hand. For Georgia, as she describes her first days in school, we see a person as enthralled with these initial experiences in learning as she is today with her college curriculum. In this segment as well as others, we see the value of building an educational foundation as well as common sense to have a successful life. The general theme points to the need to rise above external appearances such as clothes, body type, or money to nurture and praise that which comes from the inside—that which a person carries around with her, whether others can see it or not.

Georgia has moved beyond the actual land of her youth, but she can never abandon those roots nor does she want to. Of all the writers in this book, she is the narrator closest to the reader. Her language, colloquially southern, weaves her experience as well as herself as a character in phrases like "melting-in-your-mouth ready," "us youngins," or "breakfast fixin's." She invites the reader to interact with her through questions like "Why is this, you ask?" This familiarity makes reading Georgia's narrative feel like sitting on the front porch with her, sipping tea on a balmy afternoon in Louisiana. Yet Georgia still struggles to find the words to express her own experience. Her anger with standards too small and too tight for her potential remains silent in her autobiographical writing. So, like many women searching for their narrative self, Georgia continues to write and to create the story she is.

SIX

"I HAVE ARRIVED BEFORE MY WORDS"

Dionne

Unspoken Words Finally Spoken

I have arrived ahead of my words.
    When I speak there is no response.
       There is only muted silence.

My words are still not formed,
    not yet born,
       they will not be hastened or rushed.

Like one does with toy soldiers,
    I do the same with my unspoken words.
      I prop them up,
        arrange them in ranks,
         I move them about,
           caress them, cajole them.

I play games with them, these words,
    these musical games.
        In my mind I concentrate on their harmonies,
       their progression,
         but the right words
           do not form the right way
             so I push them aside.

I have arrived before my words.
   Now the words, drab, neglected,
      no longer engage me.
         The musical expression of the words
            I thought I heard
               die in the air,
                  never spoken,
                     nowhere to go.

But the pain I feel is still there,
      it's all that's left.
         It is a desert I've come to know.
            I have arrived before my words.

I want to write my story. A story so inspiring, so important to turn peoples' lives around or stop them from going down those roads I have travelled. I hope it can stop, alter, or correct someone else's life. I am not really a writer, but I am trying the best way I can to put my story on paper in hopes it turns someone else's life around. In writing, it is also letting the ghosts out of my mind.

As you approach this story, my story, it reflects a real live person, Me. My name is Dionne. My life has been played in many different acts and scenes on this journey called life. I am a Washingtonian born and bred. My complexion has been compared to the rich full color of cappuccino, accented by heartwarming brown eyes. And my smile could even outshine that great big sun high up in the sky. My strut has turned many a man's head. I'm not conceited, but it is obvious I am a descendent of the Queen of Sheba.

So often I ask myself—what is my purpose? As I sit locked in this jail cell doing my time, I have a lot of time to reflect on the choices I've made. You have the choice of which path you take, either the straight and narrow or the wide path of destruction. Life is a series of mysteries we must each unravel at our own pace. Some people solve this mystery quicker than others. Some people never do. Some like myself are still trying to put the puzzle together. Because once it is complete, I'll be complete and at peace with myself. I will be able to fulfill my destiny to be the woman the Creator intended me to be.

THIS IS MY first, no, my second time around in jail, and the more I see, the more I am determined this time not to come back. Some people act like this place is sure-nuff home. They're institutionalized. They kick off their shoes, and from their actions, you'd think this place is the Four Seasons. Even better—three hots and a cot with no bill to pay when you leave. But there is a bill to pay. It's taken out on you mentally. It can break your will, your spirit. Or you can find strength, hope, and peace of mind. During this two years of incarceration, I've come to the point to realize that this has been a life-saving, humbling experience.

When I went to jail the first time, I was scared, really afraid, so I stayed to myself. After they took my fingerprints, they took all my clothes. Then they sprayed you with lice spray everywhere, gave you a jumpsuit, and issued your prison number. They also issued you a washcloth, a towel, two sheets, one blanket, a bra, and two pairs of underwear. Then it's off to medical where they put you through various tests. By this time I was very hungry because they hadn't fed me since six in the morning. It was now nine at night. Only after they had poked, stuck, and asked me a lot of questions did they allow me to eat. Then you are shown where you can sleep.

We walked down long hallways with blacked-out windows and bars everywhere to arrive at South One which was to be my housing block for the next two months. When I got there, I was so tired I made my bed and fell in. I heard the sound of keys jingling and the echoes of bar doors in the wide hall as I drifted off to sleep. When I woke up in the morning, reality set in. I'm locked up, I thought, as the tears clouded my eyes and I asked myself the question—why me? Looking around the room, I saw two bunks and a window I couldn't see out of. Oh, how I would have appreciated the sight of a bird in flight or a tree of green leaves or even just a car going down the street.

Out of all my time incarcerated, I can say I had one close friend. Her name was Gloria. She'd get me to come out of my room and play cards. In fact, I taught her how to play a new card game. One day we were playing cards, and I was kicking it with her about what people were saying about my roommate, Diane, a white girl.

"They say she's got AIDS. Can I get it from her by using the same bathroom? I don't want to share no room with no one with AIDS," I told Gloria.

That's how ignorant I was in '92. Gloria looked at me real serious and told me that you couldn't get it like that.

"A lot of people have HIV and don't know it. Have you checked yourself out?" she asked me.

I had not checked myself, so the next day I went and took the test. About ten days later, they asked me to take another test. I will never forget when they told me I was HIV-positive. It was February 14th, 1992. Valentine's Day. The jail had me sign some papers about being tested and stated that I should get counseling, which I never got. And I needed to talk to someone. I felt desperate to tell someone. A week went by and I got real stressed out. I finally told Gloria that my test results were positive. She surprised me by saying she was positive too and had been that way since '85 from a blood transfusion.

Next couple of months rolled by and we learned a new card game, pinochle. Also we both got a job working in the laundry. We talked about AIDS, and Gloria counseled me in the best way she could about what may happen to me and what to expect. One day we were on our way to work and getting ready to leave the unit. We all used to take turns bringing snacks to eat at work. Today was my day. I had sandwiches, chips, and Kool-aid.

From out of the blue, I heard a voice shout my name, followed by, "You're going down to Lorton."

It doesn't pay to get the least bit comfortable in jail at any time. They can change all that. You just don't know the sadness that came over me when they said to pack up and I had to go.

Once I got down there, Gloria and I wrote each other a couple of times but the letters dwindled off. Gloria died two months after her release in November 1994.

I only stayed at Lorton for four months. Then I went to the halfway house where I stayed every bit of ten days. The halfway house was two houses combined. Each room was loaded with rows of double-bunked beds tightly packed together. People came and went. Some doing the right thing, others not. Someone told me it's best to stay to yourself and keep a positive attitude. When you first get there, you stay inside for seventy-two hours. I went there on a Friday and spent most of my time looking out the window anticipating when I'd get the opportunity to step over the threshold on my own. There was an excitement but also the dread of the lure of drugs. When you go out the first few days, you have to get an ID card, so I went to get my Social Security card and then a copy of my birth certificate. I got a ride from one building to another from this guy. He asked me if I wanted to get high. Even when you are trying to do the right thing, the devil sends temptation along. Well, I was strong and told him "no," got out of the car, and walked the rest of the way to my destination. It's true that if you are a recovering addict, you should not associate with people who you know use drugs. Then I talked to my boyfriend on the phone and he told me to come over to his house. When I did, he had a spread of drugs. I took one hit and it was off to the races.

The pipe was calling my name and I stayed on the run for five months. All during that time, I played deadly and dangerous games with other people's lives. People in denial do that. I got back on drugs harder than ever. I just went for it, not giving a second thought that I could be infecting others. I still had my jail fat, looking good. I needed money for drugs, so I slipped back quickly into hoe-ing around. In five short months, I lost forty-five pounds.

I always found men to take care of me. This time I had an old guy named E., a sixty-nine-year-old retired Army sergeant who liked me a lot and took me in. I didn't have to do that much, and he took good care of me. E.'s door was always open to me. But two wrongs don't make a right because he used to drink a lot. Smirnoff was his brand, while I smoked coke and snorted dope. He was an alcoholic. I was a dope fiend. A pretty young thing with her sugar daddy. One night E. spent all the money we had in the house. He had set me and himself up, but the stuff was gone about six that night. Boy, I wanted another hit bad. He said to wait until the morning and he'd go to the bank, get some money, and we could party some more. But I couldn't wait. I went out anyway, figuring I could make a little money quick and get back in the house. But I never got back because I was arrested on September 21, 1993, and have been locked up ever since. I found out he died two months later from a stroke. I hope he's with the angels. He was such a nice old man.

At one time, I was homeless for about three or four months. I lived in an abandoned house. It was during the end of winter. I had to put rags in the window to keep out the cold. I had the section I lived in secured with wooden braces for protection because it was a place people in the neighborhood came to get high. Inside my hideaway, I burned candles. People knew where to find me. One morning for some reason, I got up early and went out. It couldn't have been but a couple of hours later, the house was up in flames. When I came back, the people were glad to see me. They thought I was in the house burning up. God was watching over me. So I very well know about sleeping from pillar to post.

Right now, I'm scared. A lot of people I know who have the virus are dying. That is a constant thought on my mind. I was in denial for a long time. I have just got out of denial about seven months ago. Right now I am still healthy, but this disease is so baffling and cunning, it could kill me tomorrow. Since I've told my family I have the virus, they don't come so much or help me out by sending money. Today we had our second anniversary for our support group. In the audience was a reporter from *HIV Alive* newspaper. She liked my poem "Karen's Poem" and may publish it.

I've noticed that stress and trying to hide your illness—which is the most stressful—will affect you in a bad way. Before I joined my HIV support group, I was in deep denial. My t-count was dropping like crazy from this hiding thing. But now I feel so much better because I really don't care who knows or what they guess or speculate. I know that I'm still a human being divinely created by God and entitled to all the things the next man can have or be. The group has helped me a lot. I recommend a support group to anyone who is sick.

AS I WAS growing up, I had all the advantages materially, but the main thing I needed was love, a hug, and encouragement. Things I never got at home. That's why I left home at the age of seventeen searching for what I felt I lacked. That's when I found out that every man wants to possess a beautiful woman. Some have good intentions but some don't and I've met both.

One of the men in my life was named M. He introduced me to the pleasures of sex, the euphoria of marijuana, to the hooking [prostitution] school, and to a terrible case of crabs. What hurt the most was he said I gave the crabs to him, but how could I? He was my first lover. At the time, I was going to school half a day and working the other half. I guess after I got a taste of womanhood, I got fed up with living with my mother and her constant "this is mine," so I dropped out and worked full-time as an accounts receivable clerk. I saved my money and got my own car and a place to live. It was during this time that I went to the Go-Go and hung out at after-hours spots with my girlfriend, R.

This is when I met a different kind of man. He was older. He had his own club in Atlantic City and always sported a pocketful of money. He quickly became my sweet sugar daddy. He introduced me to snorting cocaine, drinking cognac, and oral sex which he could perform for hours and days if I let him. We had orgies that lasted for days or as long as the coke lasted with the host of other people. He would pay women to eat my pussy while he watched. He'd even provide me with a guy to fuck since he couldn't get it up. From this adventure, I got a huge nose habit and a case of venereal warts. He was a nice man though. I later found out he got shot on 9th Street trying to break up a fight.

When I think of the men in my life, one stands out because it was me who turned him out and set him on a road of destruction. J. came into my life in 1988. He provided me with a comfortable home, the use of his car, and the majority of his paycheck. He had a good job with the government making $55,000 a year and ended up shooting dope. He lost his apartment and started selling drugs on Clifford Terrace where we hung out. It took a lot to do that considering he was blonde and blue-eyed. He even started stealing and boosting [shoplifting] and eventually spent some time incarcerated in Virginia. After getting released and having no family or place to live, he and I lived in an abandoned house on 13th and Clifton for about three months. This saddened me for a long time because I showed him this road to destruction. But people have told me that he's on the right track now after being in a program for two years.

When I think about my childhood, it doesn't really start until I was about six or seven years old. I picture myself as a child with big, curious, wondering eyes, watching others joking, laughing, and playing while I, the quiet wallflower, observed from my safe haven on the wall. I wanted so very much to be a part of it all, but I was too afraid to risk my safety to venture out to join. Maybe I was afraid of not being accepted. I do remember trying and when I did, my thoughts, ideas, and questions were so tangled up that the words would always come out all mixed up. Everyone looked at me and said, "What's she trying to say?" Because of this, I never spoke unless I really had to.

When I was eight or nine, I was shown what a man's dick looks like, but it wasn't until much later that I knew that's what it was called. Even at that young age, I noticed men's attraction to me. For some reason, uncles always wanted to hold me and give me things. One uncle sticks in my mind. He wasn't my uncle at all but was my grandmother's friend who helped her make ends meet. You see, she had seven kids to raise by herself and no husband to help, so I guess they were making whoopee, too. He even started living with her. In fact, he was there when I was born because I remember my mother saying that he used to always want to hold me when I was a little baby and I always peed on him. I wonder if even then in his sick mind, he was toying with the idea of when I got older what he'd do with me.

I loved my grandmother. You had to admire the way she worked so hard to keep her family together, but I didn't admire her choice in men. Every summer I stayed at Grandma's house. I loved being there except when he was anywhere around. I always felt his eyes on me. I now know what the expression of lust looks like. Especially the time Grandma had gone out and he was there. He'd have me go to the basement and send the others to the store. He'd pull out this big black dick, make me touch it, and make me watch while he jacked off. I don't remember if he made me lick it but I am sure I'd remember if he tried to stick it in me. But nevertheless, he took away my innocence. He told me he'd whip the shit out of me if I told. So I was scared of him and I never told. It wasn't until later on that I found out that he was the father of my aunt's daughter's baby. My aunt's daughter was only fifteen years old. I think history would have repeated itself if I hadn't insisted on not going to Grandma's anymore in the summer.

To this day, I have not really told my mother how I feel. I know she was really hurt when my brother passed last year from cancer. She has that quiet kind of love because it's not ever voiced aloud. I think, though, that my mother is the most selfish person I know. She lives in her narrow world of materialism and possessions. She has never allowed me to truly love her or allowed herself to love me unconditionally. When I think of a home, I don't think of a place where love is overflowing. That is one reason I left home as soon as I could at the age of seventeen. To medicate my feelings, I started using drugs. I think writing about my mother is going to be the hardest and the best part of this story.

When I was ten, I tried to kill myself. I took a whole bottle of aspirins but nothing happened. And when I was about twelve, my mother decided she'd leave my father. I don't think there was any foresight as to what was to become of us—we didn't matter then, just like we still don't matter. So my mother left. My father started drinking more heavily. He's always been kind of weak. He was a handsome man. I believe he played around a lot, so he came home less and less as the bills grew and grew and the cupboard emptied out more and more. My brothers had their friends so they were always gone, but I was the quiet one. I didn't socialize too much and was always at home. During this period, I slept a lot.

One particular day, no one else was at home. There was no food and Daddy said he would bring some groceries with him around nine or so. When it was dark outside, he came in. I ran down the stairs because I was hungry, hoping he had some food. But there were no bags in his hand. I could smell the liquor on his breath. We were standing in the kitchen when he tried to attack me. We were wrestling on the floor. I was crying, saying, "Daddy, stop." He must have come to his senses because he rolled off of me.

It's been twenty-three years since that happened. It's been six years since I've seen him. I don't know why, but that day when I was in his company, he never looked me in the face. I don't hold any resentment, but I think he feels guilty. My brother K. is in touch with Daddy. He says Daddy is not doing so good. He's started smoking crack. He had a dump truck company in Atlanta but he's lost all his trucks. His wife left him, and they lost their house. I know how the drug life can turn your life around. I can well imagine his is upside down.

I've been locked up for a year and a half, but I still faithfully put his name on my visiting list. He still is a no-show. Dad has got to be sixty-something. I hope and pray nothing happens to him before I can get out. I have to tell him that I forgive him. Maybe that can ease some of his pain. That's probably why he started using drugs — to medicate his feelings. Maybe I didn't tell you that my father is a very handsome man. That's where I get my looks from. Mom says I walk just like him.

I THOUGHT MY drugs, my addiction, were my best and only friend. Now that I'm drug-free and my mind is clear, I can see what drugs really are and what purpose they played in the scheme of things. I thought the drugs genuinely liked me, but that's not how it was at all. Drugs just enjoy the control they have over you. I was so overwhelmed with drugs that I let them have their way with me until I became a vague resemblance to the real me. I sank deeper and deeper into the bottomless black void that is drugs. I've spent a lot of lonely depressing years with drugs. As I reflect on it, I can't remember having one happy day in drugs' company. Drugs stripped me of my creativity, my independence, my pride, my honor, and my self-esteem. I got sick and tired of the life I lived with addiction, turning tricks, misusing my body, hanging out, sometimes living in crack houses and old joints. Stealing and robbing just so I could get money so I could get a fix to feed addiction. Each fix robbed me of the true essence of me until I didn't know who I was and neither did my family or true friends. Today I am taking the stand that "I don't need drugs any more. Get away. Get out of my life." But even still that little voice, which really is yourself and the drugs, is saying, "Don't leave. Come back. Things will be different this time."

Today I finally saw the board and they granted me parole through work release. So I guess in a couple of months (that's how long they'll take to do the paperwork), I'll be actively looking for a job. Breathing fresh free air. Mr. English, my teacher, says I'm falling into relapse because I don't feel like getting up to do the stuff that I should. I've been getting depressed a lot because I'm ready to go. But then again I'm very scared. Scared I'll go back out and pick up. That will be me signing my own death warrant. I'll need some kind of support system. I wonder where that's going to come from.

DISCUSSION

Deborah Pugh

Across from the D.C. General Hospital is the D.C. Correctional Treatment Facility, a formidable fortress of ashen stone buildings with tiny windows; it appears to have burst violently from the ground below. This modern architectural labyrinth seems out of place in the settled southeast neighborhood of people, pets, and peace.

When Jeanie and I first began our classes in the jail, Dionne emerged as one of our most able and enthusiastic students. She did not participate in the various posturings of the others; if anything, she was frustrated with them for disrupting class in their attempts to control. She wanted to learn more about poetry, her favorite mode of expression, as well as other forms of writing and literature. She already had a fair collection of poetry in her cell, and she always wanted more to add to her reading list. Her love for poetry was strong and instinctive. The first thing I noticed about Dionne as a student and writer was how she *felt* the effect of words. She let them wash over her, content to let poetry work its magic without analysis or intellectualization.

I was also immediately struck by Dionne's huge, curious eyes sparkling with life—but with fragility and pain behind them. The agony of her lifelong silence speaks its own language—of a heart too kind for the world of hustlers, pushers, and tyrants. When she finally shared her words with me, I hurt to think of her giving blowjobs in alleyways and sleeping in crack houses. I couldn't imagine this beautiful poetry-lover destroying herself to fill up a deep hole left tragically early in her life.

Although Dionne had many acquaintances in jail, she always kept a wall of protection between herself and others. She was friendly and helpful with everyone, but she kept to herself—a cordial loner who loved people. At the time I met her, the walls had begun to come down, primarily because of her need to deal with her HIV infection and her participation in support groups. From conversations in class and with Dionne individually, I learned that she had never shared her life story or feelings with anyone. She labeled this "denial"; however, her reluctance to share went deeper than that. In Dionne's description of herself as a child, she is withdrawn, an "isolated wallflower" in her words. This child yearned to join others but was prevented by the fear that blocks words—the primary means of access to other people. Scientists tell us that some children are born shy. Perhaps their shyness is expressed in silent withdrawal or, like Dionne, they attempt to bridge the gulf, but the words jumble up and fail. But withdrawal from other people is the key, and Dionne has retained this coping mechanism even now in her early thirties.

The most terrifying event for a shy person is to speak in front of a group. For graduation in jail, we planned a ceremony to celebrate the words of the women. All of the female inmates, the warden, and family members were invited. Each member of the class worked for weeks selecting and practicing a piece of her writing. One of our team teachers, a specialist in performance techniques, worked with each student to hone her public speaking skills. Brother Ba, who managed the athletic program, went beyond the call of duty, setting up a stage and installing microphones on the podium and on the floor. For the final touches, he and several inmates smoked the room with burning incense, transforming the sterile green room into a hazy delight.

Dionne's nerves occasionally overcame her, but she held on this time until her moment in the spotlight. For weeks, she had practiced in between her morning job in the kitchen and her evening job at the laundry. One of the pieces she read was her "Karen's Poem," which eventually was published in the newspaper *HIV Alive*. Supportive utterings and nodding heads in the audience were evidence that the poem's subjects—drug addiction and HIV infection—touched their lives and had moved their spirits. From their applause and Dionne's reaction, it was clear that she also understood the poet's duty and power, especially in performance. For her second piece, a poem by Michelle T. Clinton, she had found a way to allow the audience to participate actively in the work. What she devised was a set of hand signals to match the words. Whenever she held up one finger, the audience would shout a word; two fingers elicited another response. The hand signals had to be perfectly orchestrated with the words in the poem to derive their full effect and meaning, and Dionne pulled it off perfectly. By the end of the poem, the audience of about forty were laughing and shouting with Dionne as their maestro.

When the readings and diploma exchange were completed, the graduating students and teachers were the first in line for cake, but I didn't see Dionne in the group. Finally, I spotted her at the other end of the room sitting alone on the speaker platform. I took her a piece of cake and praised her performance. Her response was a wall of monosyllables: a veil had fallen over her that I could not penetrate. It would be weeks before I finally learned what had happened. Dionne had invited her mother to come to her graduation, but when Dionne had arrived, her mother was not there. She called, and her mother said she was ready and walking out the door and would be there in twenty minutes. But she never showed up, and Dionne was devastated. She would remain like this for weeks, and I never saw her recover that passion and zeal for her work again.

Students like Dionne challenge teachers to provide their very best. However, in the class at jail, it was often difficult, usually impossible, to spend more than five uninterrupted minutes with one student. To arrange time outside of class was nearly impossible. Visiting hours were an option, but my schedule was already strained to the limit, and the noisy furor of visiting rooms was not conducive to an intense discussion of her writing. So mostly we wrote letters to each other—some mailed through the post, some passed on Monday nights. It was through these letters that Dionne wrote her story.

WHEN I INITIALLY spoke with Dionne about writing her memoir for this book, she was at first surprised and then delighted. It was only later that she realized how difficult it would be to wrestle with her silences. As her editor, I put together pieces of her letters and returned them to her with extensive notes and suggestions. She was astonished to read her own words, and although we discussed my notes—which for the most part asked her to dig deeper into her experiences—she never gave me a rewrite.

Dionne's first question about writing her story was "where do I begin?" Although this question is part of all writing, the most powerful influence on the autobiographical writer's choice of memories, plotting, and characterization is her present situation. Because of Dionne's fairly recent involvement with support groups, she found herself for the first time opening up and sharing incidents of her life with other people. And in a support group as well as autobiography, the underlying question is: How did I get from there in my past to here in my present?

From the first page of her writing, Dionne says her purpose is threefold: she is writing her story to help other people, to let the ghosts out of her mind, and to put the puzzle pieces of her life together. Tearing open the mask of secrets was very difficult for Dionne; probably the only way she could muster the strength to do so was through the lens of contrition. The writing she offers is thus a story of redemption, perhaps less for herself than for someone else. Yet there is an underlying sense in her writing of inevitability. It is as if she fears in her secret heart that putting the pieces together will not ensure that there will be completeness and peace, even though her most desperate hope is that this is the key to unraveling the mystery of her addiction.

In her selection of memories, Dionne attempts to determine what made her the person she is. However, there is far more hidden in her selections than revealed. Only two remembrances—her first day in jail and her friendship with Gloria—are specific, detailed memories. The section on her first day in jail is the only place where she allows herself to relive the actual experience, relating it in narrative form with sensual details like "blacked-out windows," "the sound of keys jingling," "the echoes of bar doors," and the feeling of loss at not being able to see "a bird in flight or a tree of green leaves." In recalling her friendship with Gloria, the use of dialogue allows the reader and, more important, Dionne access to the real, lived experience.

But the rest of Dionne's memoir suggests that the primary way she views herself is in relation to drugs. Her addiction provides the controlling theme for nearly everything else she writes, and the predominance of that theme severely limits the way she presents her story. In the scenes about her family and the men in life, her writing branches away from specific detail into memories involving the theme of her addiction. In her support groups, disclosing these memories was her first attempt to explode denial. But as important as the shedding of secrets is, it is only the first step in the process of recovering a life.

The greatest struggle for Dionne in confronting her story is the pressure to use only those experiences that support the drug theme. I do not mean to imply that this is a conscious choice for Dionne, for certainly it is not, but a person caught in destructive personal myths has a tendency to magnify the negative and entirely forget the positive aspects of her past. Thus, Dionne fills page after page illustrating her role in her path to destruction, yet she writes only two lines about her achievements: getting a job as an accounts receivable clerk, saving her money, purchasing a car, and renting an apartment at seventeen years old. She quickly sacrifices the child with "big, curious, wondering eyes" to the wallflower, without applying the introspection and speculation necessary to understand what forces came together to silence that child. She calls her relationship with her mother the "best part of this story," yet in spite of my encouragement she never writes it.

To break this silencing, the autobiographical writer needs to return to her experiences and write about them in as much detail as possible. Although no memory is entirely accurate, striving for accuracy helps the writer get to the bottom of her memories intellectually and, more important, emotionally. For Dionne, this narrative reliving may produce forgotten facts or evidence that can help her see her life has a larger meaning than simply her connection with drugs.

In her conception of herself as the beautiful woman men want to possess, Dionne defines herself as object, but it becomes apparent that the men also exist as objects for her. She describes them as mostly "sweet sugar daddies"—with the exception of her "uncle" who molested her; she has, in fact, startlingly perceptive insights about him. She resolutely longs for connections with other people that never happen—especially her mother (whom she calls "the most selfish person I know") and her father (whose clumsy attempt to attack her long ago is still vivid in her mind, but does not keep her from putting his name on her visitor list at jail, hoping he will visit so she can tell him she forgives him). There is no more poignant line in Dionne's story than this one: "When I was ten, I tried to kill myself . . . but nothing happened." She was obviously unsuccessful in her suicide attempt, but she also seems to suggest that her cry for help generated no response, perhaps even no acknowledgment.

In the absence of genuine human connections, is it any surprise that drugs become, as she says, her "best and only friend"? She personifies drugs throughout her story: the pipe calls her name; drugs "liked" her; drugs stripped her of her creativity, independence, pride, honor, and self-esteem; and even now, drugs whisper to her, "Don't leave. Come back. Things will be different this time." Part of this language comes from Alcoholics Anonymous and Narcotics Anonymous, but her words clearly demonstrate how she has projected her desires onto this one object.

The fact that Dionne is so much more than the story of her addiction is only glimpsed in her autobiography, yet it shines through in her poetry. Her dance with poetry was a clear attempt at loving and giving voice to the life force within her. In the first two stanzas of her poem "Unspoken Words Finally Spoken," she seems to be split between the poet of her soul and the silencing taskmaster of her intellect. She is tortured because the poet is enlightened and has full knowledge of the split; what agony is worse than to be aware of what will destroy and yet be powerless to stop it? In the third stanza, the words as toy soldiers evoke dual images. In one, Dionne is the master strategist, the commanding general in a mock battle, although the game is still one of the coexistence of life and death. Yet, in the other image, just as toy soldiers are impotent representations of real soldiers in battle, Dionne somehow knows that her words at this point are still lifeless representations of her inner emotions. Yet she continues to caress and cajole them.

The fourth stanza presents the realization of the creative, where Dionne is once again the child with curious, wondering eyes. However, she also allows her enemy, judgment, into the fantasy, and the "right words do not form the right way so I push them aside." Imagination and hope are vanquished, and the pain returns not because the words do not exist but because she has prejudged the quality of her words (and herself) and will not speak them for fear they will not be heard. Once again, the poet of the soul is defeated, and in the final stanza, life becomes a desert where words shrivel before they are born.

As I reflect on both Dionne's poetry and her love of reading others' poetry, I wish I had asked her to write her autobiography as an epic poem. Perhaps that form of expression could have opened up her story to her, producing the emotional catharsis needed to bring about healing. Dionne's autobiographical writing did offer her some relief from the past as the pain begins to appear in expressed language: the words do make it to the page. However, much of Dionne's struggle to get rid of her ghosts and put her puzzle together still seems located in addiction rather than encompassing the whole mosaic of her life.

Although the shape of a person's autobiography tends to center around the present, understanding addiction is incomplete if the only focus is on the addiction itself. Most of Dionne's memories are tied to the feeling of shame—a debilitating emotion because not only does it create feelings of worthlessness and inferiority, but it causes one to conceal oneself from and withdraw from other people. This withdrawal results in a feeling of invisibility that then prevents one from achieving the connections that are so desperately needed.

In Dionne's failure to access and accept all of herself, both good and bad, there is a loss of completeness. The more you know Dionne, the more troublesome it is to understand how someone so full of life could be so set on extinguishing it. Yet, in Dionne's case, transcendence is no simple matter. In many ways, Dionne's personal story is overcome by society's narrative. She has played almost all negative roles available to women—drug addict, prostitute, and vamp. In the process, she has internalized self-loathing, repressed her words, and denied herself the right to a full emotional existence. In her writing, we see echoes of fear, sorrow, and shame, but curiously, no anger. Instead of expressing her anger outwardly, Dionne has turned it back into herself—going beyond the limits of invisibility and into the realm of self-destruction.

SEVEN

"CREATIVITY HAS GOT TO FIND AN EXPRESSIVE CHANNEL SOMEHOW"

Angie

I am no longer homeless, but I have been through the experience. I write this in the beginning days of 1996, and have had my own shelter since the summer of 1992. The aftershocks of having been homeless would still come back to haunt me just until the recent past. I still feel a shudder now and then. To be alone without one of life's basic requirements—shelter—is a traumatic event.

I define homelessness as not having a roof over one's head to call her own—in other words, the lack of a physical space to call home. But at least for me, there was an added dimension to being homeless. I experienced an internal feeling of emptiness, an aching that at times felt like it would never, ever go away. It was like a living puzzle: how did I get in this predicament anyway? This catastrophe wasn't supposed to happen to *me*.

In the spring of 1991, I had to give up a large, two-bedroom apartment in which I had lived for twenty-two years. I had reared my two sons there, first as a working single parent and then as an unemployed disabled mother trying to eke out an existence on extremely limited means. My sons helped by working summers. As they grew into fine adults, they continued to help. However, I had raised them to value independence and did not want them to feel that they were obligated to spend the rest of their lives living with me and helping to support me.

151

I could no longer postpone the inevitable. I couldn't pay the rent. I would have to move. I think that I was in a state of shock for a while.

I had become disabled after a bout with breast cancer in 1973. Complications developed from the radiation therapy, and I spent six months in the hospital. When I physically recovered from radiation burns, I would from time to time smile a little to myself and wonder just how "therapeutic" it had been in the face of the ensuing physical damage and disability. Also, during those years, I suffered the periodic psychotic episodes associated with manic-depressive illness. Usually I was depressed. I had been hospitalized for mental illness several times, but was not correctly diagnosed until 1992 after my homeless experience. In that year, I was finally placed on the correct medication and continued psychotherapy. Today, I am stabilized, balanced, feeling more in control of myself and what concerns me; I am looking forward to the future.

I have been asked what in my opinion made the difference between me and others who are still homeless, living in shelters or on the streets, caught up in a cycle of despair with seemingly no hope for anything better in the future. I suppose I could get philosophical or wordy about it, but simply put, someone very close to me once said that I was "lucky." I told her that I choose to think of it as being blessed.

I have an active prayer life, though I'm not often on my knees or in church that regularly. I do now, and have for a long time, made a practice of turning my life over to the loving care of God; relaxing in order to be receptive to those tuggings of spirit in which the answers come; listening for guidance to action. For example, one day in 1989, before I even knew I would have to move, I decided to apply for public housing. Something like my intuition told me that I should just apply, so I signed up on the list. I am so glad I heeded this inner voice.

During the three-year waiting period, I lost the old apartment and entered into a period of homelessness that lasted for fifteen months. I didn't know where I was going to stay until about two or three days before I had to vacate the apartment that had been my home for so many years. I stayed with a neighbor who lived a block away. She had a small but lovely art gallery downstairs in her house. I felt at home there, but I moved after a couple of months. I then went to the suburbs to stay with long-time friends. Here too I felt at home, but I didn't want to wear out my welcome. I would eventually move five times in this year and a half. Although I was never without a roof over my head, I felt rootless, moving from place to place, staying with friends and acquaintances in D.C. and the nearby suburbs. When would all this, as my elders said when I was a child, "living from pillar to post" come to an end?

In addition to the loss of my home and the realities of living with a physical disability in which I could no longer use my right arm, I had not yet been correctly diagnosed for severe manic-depression. I'm glad now that I had enough clarity then to understand that I needed help. In other words, I admitted I had a problem and took the necessary steps to remedy the situation. I wanted a life without all the crippling mental highs and lows of the illness. I wanted to feel balanced between the two, to be stable. To be normal, I guess.

The waiting period for public housing was just about up when I was called to come and look at a vacancy. I liked it. I moved in, and that was July 1992. Since then, I have been in my own space again for almost four years. I like the feeling. I want to enjoy God's gift of life after all the physical and mental health challenges. I have survived to enjoy the blessing of life as opposed to cursing it. For me, it is all about living life one day at a time, making the most of it, and yes, loving it.

A new season dawns
Now, a sunny place
   and space
of her own—after a season of streets.
Yes, a light at the end of the tunnel—
   it is not a speeding train.
Welcome home, Serenity,
Welcome home, Peace—
A place to call my own.

I FIRST BECAME aware of myself as a creative person when I was a child in school. I had to design a house for an art class. I made the house out of very lightweight cardboard and Plexiglas. The Plexiglas was used to give the front and dining rooms a curved, sweeping view of the outside. I recall the feeling of connectedness with my inner, personal world and the feeling of being at peace with myself, of being able to use what I had available to express my inner vision. I owe this desire to see everyday things in out-of-the-ordinary ways to my mother and father, now physically deceased. Their artistic and spiritual eyes live on in me. I use the raw material of their genes to express my vision in my own way.

My father was an artist who painted in oils. In every place he ever lived, he always painted an original design on the kitchen floor. He fixed airplane engines for a living. He would bring airplane parts home and fashion them into things for use around the house. He also created stainless steel sculpture out of these spare parts. He used to say to me, "Everything real is invisible." By that he meant that everything that we see in the material world started as an *idea* in somebody's mind, and through whatever medium the artist chose to use, this idea was presented as a creation to her world.

My father was a sort of oddball, I gather, from the time he was a little boy. He was born in 1921. He came from a family of nine siblings. He used to tell me how they always thought he was strange because he wore his hair long and in two braids. This was on a farm somewhere in Georgia or northern Florida. He cut his hair off when he was twelve. There were Native Americans in the family. I don't know which tribe, and that's something I would love to know more about. He was just always the sort of guy who did his own thing. He taught himself to play the piano. Just knowing his sisters and brothers from when I was growing up, I can imagine how different he must have been. I always felt I was different, too.

My father was a very spiritual person, as opposed to being a religious man. As he got older, he started studying metaphysics and spirituality. On my wall here, I have a portrait my father did of me when I was younger. I didn't sit for it. He did it as a surprise. When

I first saw it, I had the feeling, oh God, my father really knows me. He painted me without my shoes on, and I love that because I was always going around the house barefoot. When he let me see it for the first time, he asked about this little pennant painted into the portrait. I guess I had some feeling back then that I might not get out of the University of the District of Columbia because when he asked what school name he should put on the pennant, I asked him to write Dunbar (my high school). My minister told me he put things that have spiritual significance—a candle and parrot and cat—in the portrait to protect me. I never had to know, really, why he put them there, and it never occurred to me to ask him. I just knew him, and it seemed like something he would do.

I used to think of my father as the creative one. I always recognized my mother's skill as a seamstress, but I thought her gift was more technical than spiritual or creative. I see now that she was creative as well. She was just a whiz at doing all kinds of technical things. Her sewing, reweaving, and other craft skills had the look of a pro, not an amateur. My mother frequently worked at dry cleaners because she didn't earn that much from sewing for private customers. She worked in these dry cleaning establishments doing alterations and so forth. Back in the early '60s, she went to work at a place that had a reweaving component to its alteration business. They taught her to reweave, and she learned how to do that really well. I mean, she could reweave holes left by burns and cuts in her-ringbone tweeds so that one couldn't see the damage at all.

One of the cleaners she was working for when President Johnson was in the White House was located on 14th Street and New York Avenue, NW. They've torn the old place down, and it is now a tall, modern office building. Apparently, someone in the White House called one day wanting a seamstress to come and do alterations for the Johnson ladies. Now, my mother was not the type to get all excited about these things. She had to get a security clearance and go through all the red tape. She went down and presented her ID to the guard at the gate, and he let her in. She would go there from time to time to do alterations on President Johnson's clothes. It was a great experience for her. I wrote that into her obituary when she died a few years ago.

She was a perfectionist and taught me to be a perfectionist—not that that was necessarily a good thing. When I was little and she was teaching me how to sew, she would rip apart anything I did that didn't meet her high standards. I think that it created in me a reluctance to try new things. I worried it just would never be good enough. I gained a lot of my general attitude of self-acceptance from what my father instilled in me as a creative girl child. He accepted me as I was—that I was okay just as I was. The things that I produced for him were just fine; no need for my work to be torn up and devalued. I sometimes feel that emotionally I'm balancing between their lessons of Okay/Not Okay.

My parents separated when I was about twelve. My brother and I moved to a new apartment with my mother, while my father stayed in our old place in southwest Washington. So I find myself when I'm talking about things, saying, oh yeah, that happened before or after the family split up.

There was a lot of pain in my relationship with my mother. We spent, I'd say, more time not talking than we did talking to each other. She had so much pain that she hadn't worked out and grieving she hadn't done that she transferred a lot of that anger onto me. As far as her relationship with me was concerned, she didn't talk a lot about her past. I have a cousin that she talked to sometimes, and that's how I found out some of the things I've learned since she died. She would talk to other people, and she had a kind of sharing relationship with her cousins, the ones she grew up with after her mother was hospitalized. I'm not saying she had to want to tell everything to everybody, but with me she was so secretive. She didn't have a therapist or anybody like that to whom she could tell all these things. You know, nothing is so bad that you can't tell somebody. Otherwise, it starts to do some terrible things to the person who is holding the secret.

I'm sure that I was my mother's worst nightmare realized because not only was I born a female, I was someone she'd have to guard and watch like a hawk. I ended up getting pregnant at sixteen anyway; and then, in my early twenties, I started to show symptoms of mental illness. I was, I think, a lot of the time a re-embodiment of her mother because of the legacy of mental illness. My mother had so much emotional anguish concerning *her* mother's situation—she had been in a mental hospital—and she had kept it a secret from us. Also, my mother had married young because she too had gotten pregnant. I was a living reminder of some painful memories. For many years, this kept us apart, both emotionally and physically.

My mother had a lot of defense mechanisms in place, like her work, to cope with unresolved memories. She was a workaholic just like my father and, to some extent, my brother too. I think that's how they've dealt with their pain. By working so hard, they never had to get too close to it. Emotionally speaking, I didn't want to be like my mother. I was angry at her for years, although I recognized early on that my mother was a very talented woman. For a long time, one of the earliest memories I had of my mother was her with her back to me. I was a little girl, and she was sitting at the sewing machine with her back to me. I have a memory of watching my father paint with his back to me too. It was like I didn't matter. They had just shut me out.

It hasn't been until the recent past, until she died in 1988, that I would let feelings come up and think about things and do what I needed to do to have painful memories move on and see it another way. I went to the Textile Museum in 1994 on the sixth anniversary of my mother's death because I didn't want to go to the cemetery but wanted to acknowledge it in some way. The Textile Museum is not very far from where she used to live. I strolled around there and looked at the tapestries and so forth and felt like I was reconnecting with some of her spirit. I see now that I am a lot like her. I have that same courage to endure. You know, she was always so absorbed.

Bringing back that early childhood memory of them with their backs to me has really helped me a lot. Now I see two creative people who were involved, totally absorbed in what they were doing. It has been healing to get to that realization. In that healing, I realize that she could not give to me the maternal nurturing that she herself did not receive as a child. I know in my heart that she loved me. I am quite comfortable with that certainty.

The two years she lived after my brother died were very hard for her. I know she suffered terribly with the death of her son. It must have been a very difficult thing. I mean, I lost a child too, but I never saw that child. Now I have had the benefit of some years of therapy and have made a lot of peace with myself about the pain and the anger and the rage that I felt towards my mother. I had never talked to her in detail about all that separated us, but it affected the way I related to her. I'm glad I had some sense of peace and healing about our silence.

I REMEMBER A photograph I had taken of me on the balcony in the sixth grade. It was of this chubby little girl. In my adult life, I have struggled with my addiction to food, and I'm pretty clear my eating disorder started when I was about ten years old. I feel I began to use food as an expression of the confusion and rage I experienced because, at this time, I was sexually abused by an older teenage stepcousin. I was maybe eight or nine years old.

When I came into adolescence and started growing up, I thought: what did I do to make him do that? And I didn't do anything at all. It's all very confusing, but the terrible part is that none of this is happening at a conscious level. I binged and grew rounder and rounder, and for ten years I told nobody at all. Then I told my mother, but she didn't say anything to indicate she believed me. I waited for almost another twenty years to talk to her about it again; at that time, she finally believed me and was very supportive.

I would venture so far as to say that a lot of overweight women are suffering from the effects of childhood sexual abuse and, by consequence, from the rage that goes deeper than outrage. There's also the need to fend off people, and especially men, from bothering you; you turn them off. I guess I would say it's about trying to control your space. You pad yourself so you don't have to worry about any guys bothering you. I couldn't seem to express that rage any other way, so I binged. It's a complex response: sometimes it was about medicating myself so I didn't hurt, so that I didn't feel any emotional pain. Food became a very immediate sort of way to distract and medicate myself.

It's not until talking to somebody, if you're inclined to do so, that you can start to gradually unravel some of the rage and shame and sadness you experienced both as a child and an adult. In my family, we didn't talk about things this way. We were a family of addicts as a way to express those things we couldn't or wouldn't say. My brother was a workaholic, just like my mother and father, and I used food. I've heard people in OA (Overeaters Anonymous) meetings say they eat when they're sad and they eat when they're glad. So often, you'll be shocked that this or that woman, when she seems to have it all together, has this intense, troubled personality. But maybe she's got something going on inside that she just hasn't talked about.

I've been doing some thinking about the statistics I've seen recently that state that almost 50 percent of black women are overweight. And I wonder a lot about what that's all about. I think it has something to do with the stress of having to cope in a racist world. And, too, we live in a world where the media projects all these idealized images at you, that this is what you're supposed to look like. So much of that struggle gets internalized. I get so angry when those commercials come on television for those weight-loss clinics. They just want to make money off of women's misery. You know, just bring me your money. I turn it off because I don't want to hear it.

I WAS SIXTEEN years old when I got married because I was pregnant with that first child, the girl. Looking back, I believe that to be the time of my first serious depression. I was sixteen, pregnant, and unmarried. I also had to drop out of high school in the first half of my senior year; besides, my mother was very unhappy about the whole situation. It was a horrible time. I did go back to high school

and graduate, but at the time I thought I was in love. The baby died
from congenital defects half an hour after her birth.

Later, when I got home from the hospital, I would ask myself
and God, "If I got married because I was pregnant, and my baby
died, should I stay married?" I didn't get married because I was
madly in love. At sixteen years old and pregnant, what do you know
about all these other luxuries like being madly in love? Well, I said
to myself, I'm married, so I guess I'll stay married. So I stayed married for nine and a half years.

When I got pregnant a second time, I went to great lengths to
find a private OB/GYN because I didn't want to subject myself to
being a staff patient in a public hospital again. I didn't have to that
time because I had health insurance. Anyway, I made great plans to
be put to sleep. I started into labor on January 30, 1960, very early
in the morning. I called my doctor and told him what was going on,
and he said, come on to the hospital. We didn't have a car at that
time, so we called for a cab a couple of times, but it never got there,
so my husband went down the hill to hail a cab. He brought the cab
back to the apartment. At that time we lived a full flight of stairs
down into the basement. By this time the labor pains were pretty
hard, and I had to climb that full flight of stairs to get outside and
into the cab. I managed to do that, and we were sailing along until
we got near the hospital and my water broke. The cab driver was
an elderly man who was very nervous. I was leaning on my husband's shoulder, and he was fussing at the cab driver. It was a Saturday morning and there was no traffic to speak of, but the cab
driver was stopping to wait for red lights to turn green. And my
husband was saying, "Why are you stopping? Why are you stopping? She's going to have this baby!" The cab driver called his dispatcher to tell him there was a lady in the back of the cab about to
have a baby and what should he do. So the dispatcher's office noti-
fied the hospital that we were on the way and to please meet us in
the back at the emergency entrance.

We got there, but the water had already broken and the baby had
started to come out. He was born to his waist, and I could still feel

his feet fluttering inside me, and he was crying. And I was fully clothed. I had on a winter coat, a maternity dress, a blouse, under-clothes, everything. The nurses and doctor on call were at the back waiting for us, and we finished delivery in the back of the cab. They wrapped the baby up in a sheet and took him into the hospital. He went into the hospital before I did! After they got me into the hos-pital and into a bed, I wanted to know when I could go home. I felt really good. I later talked to my doctor and asked him if I would get a refund because I had my baby in the cab! I didn't.

The reason I'm telling this story is because it made a difference from thereafter in how I felt about myself as a woman. I was able to give birth almost unassisted. It had a really profound impact on me because I had the baby without drugs and without any help to speak of. I mean it said a lot for the baby too because he pretty much delivered himself. I think childbirth toughens a woman in some spiritual, unseen way. It did me. I felt that if I could survive *that* experience, then I could survive anything. That feeling of confidence was something that was in my life for a long time. It was like some-thing wonderful inside that was quietly kept.

A major depression in 1965 landed me in the hospital when my baby was two months old. When the baby was seven months old, I separated from my husband. I was twenty-five years old and thought I had seen the worst of it, emotionally speaking. My husband died fourteen months later, a young man of twenty-eight years. He suc-cumbed to a cerebral hemorrhage, complications from congenital kidney disease, and hypertension. The children were six years and twenty-one months old. This was in 1966.

It was after I had this third child that I went through my first serious depression and had to be hospitalized. In those days, you just didn't hear a lot about postpartum depression. I never wanted to die. I just sort of wanted to escape to where I wouldn't be so stressed out. I had a therapist tell me once that I was not the sort of woman who depended on my children for a sense of self, and I had never given it a lot of thought, but it's true.

After my youngest son turned three months old, I went back to work. You know, I love my children dearly, but it was this feeling I had to get out in the world to make money and be an adult working woman. I tried to raise my children in a way that they would feel free to explore life and find out who they were for themselves, quite apart from any designs I might have had for them. I had two sons to raise as a single parent, wondering how I was going to pay the rent from month to month. I tried to raise them in such a way that the day-to-day situations wouldn't impact negatively on their lives. We still had contact with my family, although there was no real support system. My emotional support system usually consisted of friends outside the family.

One day in late August 1973 while taking a shower, I discovered a lump in my right breast. It was about the size of the large end of an egg. It was long before mammograms became a matter of routine for women of a certain age. I was young, however, only thirty-three. I went to a doctor in the oncology department of a local hospital for an examination. He aspirated it: put a needle in the lump to see if it was filled with fluid. When it wasn't, he suggested that I check into the hospital to have a biopsy.

I was frightened, anxious, and for all practical purposes, alone. I was an unemployed, widowed parent with two wonderful sons at thirteen and eight years old. They would have to be my main support system. I would have to be their support system as well. I'm sure that they were as frightened as I.

By the time I got everything arranged for my stay in the hospital, it was approaching the middle of September 1973. In those days, women were not offered the options as far as what to do if one had breast cancer. I signed consent forms giving the surgeons permission to remove my breast during the procedure (while I was under anesthesia) should the lump prove malignant.

The partial outcome of this is that I woke up from the anesthesia all bandaged up on my upper right side. I was told by a recovery room nurse that I had had a radical mastectomy. Furthermore, after sustaining severe radiation burns that caused an infection, I had six skin graft surgeries to repair the damage to my chest and armpit. I was hospitalized for six months. During that time, I lost the use of my right arm. The radiation and all of the grafting damaged the nerves in my armpit. I have what is called a brachial plexus injury.

After this, I was very depressed. Confined to bed for most of that time with my right arm in traction, I was unable to talk to my sons even by phone. The nearest phone was in the hallway, and I couldn't get out of bed to walk to it. I saw my sons once in the six months I was hospitalized, and that was when the homemaker aide brought them to my room. I was in a large ward. The elder one could come to my bedside. The younger one had to stand in the doorway to the ward. I waved to him. He waved back to me. I missed them so much.

Since these operations in 1974, I have been permanently disabled. Many people have asked me if I sued for malpractice. I didn't sue, primarily because of being seriously depressed from being in the hospital and after being discharged. I had no one to advise me about the statute of limitations. Several years had passed before the depression lifted and I looked into the possibility of filing a suit. By then, it was too late.

My sons and I had to make it the best way that we could on what little we had coming in. We did make it, and they are now commendable young men, married and with families of their own. Between both of them and my daughters-in-law, they have given me five beautiful granddaughters. Truly, my sons have given me daughters.

DEPRESSION, IN THE past, has been my prison. Thank God that is no longer the case. I have learned from my own experiences and those of others that many women suffer from manic-depressive illness. Being clinically depressed for so many years was like being separated, shut out (or in), isolated behind an invisible wall. It's a peculiar variety of torture because it looks as though one is part of society—an active member taking part in everyday activities—but one is effectively locked away behind a barrier that is a product of one's brain chemistry. I have sometimes thought that some of the depression in women that is so widespread in all levels of our society might be related to trying to cope with and adjust to living in a patriarchal system.

I could usually tell when something was going wrong—delusional thinking and hallucinations and all the stuff—and would check myself into a hospital. I've had nearly every kind of psychotropic drug known to man, but I kept getting sick. I wasn't always in therapy, but when I was hospitalized I would talk to therapists. So it wasn't until about 1992 that they discovered I had been misdiagnosed all these years. The incorrect diagnoses were everything from schizophrenia, depression, schizo-affective disorder, mixed personality disorder, some of everything.

I continue to have bouts of depression, but it doesn't incapacitate me the way it once did. It has taken a lot of counseling, and I continue to trust in God. I've been correctly diagnosed with manic-depression and have finally been put on the proper medication. With manic-depressive disorder, you have these euphoric highs and these crashing lows, and my high periods never lasted very long, maybe two or three days. Now I've been in therapy for a while with the same person, and she has really helped me deal with a lot of stuff that I don't know I could have come through alone.

When I first started taking lithium three years ago, I had to get through some side effects. I used to do a lot of things creatively. I used to sew; my mother taught me at an early age. In high school, I'd make clothes for my home ec teacher's child. I learned how to sew from making doll clothes from these patterns my mother would buy for me. I used to crochet and took tap dance lessons and had this camera I wanted to learn to use. Before the tumor in my breast was discovered, I was taking guitar lessons. After the loss of my right arm, I was not able to do these things anymore. I would try to sew with one hand or play the guitar, but it just didn't feel the same, so I put it all aside. I know a lot of people don't like to take lithium because it interferes with their creativity, and it took me awhile to adjust to the changes in my brain chemistry.

I've gotten used to life in this middle zone, this neutral zone, without the euphoric highs or crashing lows. I was used to feeling really up or really down, and I could see why some people don't want to take it because the lithium just sort of has you in a neutral zone. But now I don't feel that way. I think that everyone has access to creativity. You express it in different ways. I taught myself to write with my left hand, and I am learning to be a better writer. It seems that creativity has got to find an expressive channel somehow.

THE POWERFUL FEELINGS of the trauma of grief can be a purifying, healing, and transforming experience. It takes as long as it takes; it cannot be rushed. At times, it seems that the knowledge that it will end is the only thing that gets one through the day. My mother, father, and brother are all gone completely to spirit now, but through imagination I visit them even as I grow older and time passes on.

This creativity comes from the Creator. I am a speck in the heart and mind of the God who has given me the ability to express myself artistically. Even in my darkest moments of depression, my faith never disappeared completely. I continued to believe in the possibility of being and feeling well and whole; to believe in the possibility of healing; that the Creator was there for me, waiting, prodding, gently coaxing me back to health. I feel blessed to be at a place in my life where I am exploring new ways to be that expressive woman. I feel that most people have access to creative self-expression; we each just express our gifts in different ways and mediums.

Writing is a way for me to clarify and organize some of my thoughts and feelings about my life and healing process. It has been an emotionally and physically tumultuous life with many traumas, highs and lows, and resting stops along the way. The writing is therapeutic, a very important part of the ongoing process of healing and reconnecting with the whole and creative female that I think I was at the outset.

With the disability cutting me off from creative self-expression in the forms I was accustomed to, I started to try my left hand more at writing. Teaching myself to write with my left hand was a major challenge, but I'm glad that I stuck with it. I'm proud of my left-handed script. When I had mastered control of my left hand, I started to do more creative writing, mostly poetry. I found it a great outlet for some of the frustration and stress I felt after becoming disabled.

The creative writing has helped me to actually *be* creative again as opposed to morosely musing about the nature of creativity. The years since my breast cancer operation have gotten me in touch with the fact that I am basically a creative woman who, when familiar avenues are cut off, has to find other means of artistic self-expression. It is necessary for my survival.

I have, in a sense, come home into my own serenity and peace.

DISCUSSION

Jeanie Tietjen

I knock on the ground floor window of the stone apartment building where Angie lives, less than fifteen blocks from the U.S. Capitol.

"Is there a poet in the house?"

"I'm coming, just hold on a minute. Let me turn off this TV."

I hear her feet deliberately dropping and lifting, and she opens the door. I have a sack of bread, salad, and diet Coke. She turns down the green-painted hall, and I follow her into the apartment.

I first met Angie at the Dinner Program for Homeless Women. Linda, the program director, introduced her to me before class one afternoon. In social service programs, one is visited by a lot of social and psychiatric workers, reporters, philanthropists, all in search of the defining experiences of homelessness. But Angie was primarily interested in talking not about homelessness, but rather the creative possibilities of women together—how we can heal each other through speaking and listening. She impressed me from the first moment with her ability to listen, to intuit and respond.

Her presence in our writing workshop has been a gift: she is faithful, consistent, and supportive. Part of what she supplies is a voice trained on the interior narrative. She emphasizes through her writing and her comments that what one experiences internally, genuinely, is the heart of any story. This insistence shapes her impact on the class.

Her effect on me was especially powerful because she is just a year or two away in age from my mother, and between their lives and mine, worlds open. What seemed revolutionary to their generation is nearly unquestioned in mine. For a woman to work, for example, to have a self outside the role of wife and mother were new ideas in the years Angie and my mother were making crucial decisions when relatively young. By getting to know Angie, I felt I was gaining familiarity with a legion of women who made the life I live possible.

Angie has been living since 1992 in this one-bedroom apartment, which she's decorated with jars of dried flowers, patterned cloths, and pillows. Her father's portrait of her hangs by the front door. Taped to the wall is a collection of crayon sketches by her granddaughters. On the table outside the kitchen, she has rolled out two placemats. As we catch up on what's happened to each of us since we last met, she sets plates and napkins on the table, using her one "good" arm, her left hand pushing aside poems and transcripts she has been editing.

We have dinner and talk and then put a cassette in the tape recorder to document her unfolding life story. Angie's voice is touched with something of the South, her Florida roots splaying into words that gradually, over the passing seasons, have sounded out her sense of the past fifty or so years. The passage from the inner theater to the remembering voice refashions what is past into her current world. The voice does not merely report a tidy file of consecutive occurrences; it exclaims over a "lost" memory, weaving long-ago events into the present life, forging a narrative relationship between the woman and her past. In retrieving a life through telling, then writing, she stakes a present claim against a sense of loss. Writing "I remember" is akin to saying "I survive."

Angie's memoir is especially important in the context of this book because it sheds light on the complex dimensions of homelessness. One does not lose shelter, family, finances, and survival network overnight. The phrase many use that homelessness is "one paycheck away" illustrates the tenuous line between poverty and homelessness, underlining it as an economic condition. In its everyday usage, this phrase good-heartedly attempts to undo the stigma associated with homelessness, to take the blame out of the matter. This empathic gesture, however, often falls short of the larger picture because its implicit remedy is economic, and homelessness is not exclusively a matter of money. As Angie writes:

> But at least for me, there was an added dimension to being homeless. I experienced an internal feeling of emptiness, an aching that at times felt like it would never, ever go away. It was like a living puzzle: how did I get in this predicament anyway?

Angie's life story correlates emotional and physical disability with unemployment, poverty, and the loss of her home and thus unravels many facets of homelessness, including material privation. But as a whole, the story documents losses wound into the isolation and chaos she experienced by marking those points at which the physical worlds of poverty and homelessness collided with the psychological. It illuminates her descent, but the text itself witnesses recovery, at each turn transforming a fragment of loss into the body of her survival story. Angie's text is a deliberate map through which she recovers a sense of herself. It is, as she once remarked, as if writing her life story was, in a sense, coming home.

Angie's narrative voice celebrates life, although this stance should not obscure her pain and suffering nor the tenacity it took for her to survive. Nevertheless, her life story, as it appears in this book, assures a "happy ending" from its earliest pages:

> I am no longer homeless, but I have been through the experience. . . .
>
> . . . I have survived to enjoy the blessing of life as opposed to cursing it. For me, it is all about living life one day at a time, making the most of it, and yes, loving it.

She shares a story of manic-depressive illness, childhood sexual abuse, poverty, loss of her first child, loss of the father of her two boys, breast cancer, a permanent disability, and many years of significant grief in the context of a persistent faith and belief in her own creativity. She has earned this authorial stance and confers its message of survival, so that others might find themselves in her struggle—especially other women, and most especially other black women.

WE STAND SIDE by side in her tiny kitchen. There's a jar of spaghetti sauce and one of mustard that Angie cannot open with her one "good" hand. Usually, her disability is so well-integrated into her life that I don't see it. At moments such as this, I am acutely aware of her disabled hand and arm, the right one, rendered so by post-mastectomy treatments. I notice how little I notice, and in this instant, I feel how much I take for granted. Putting on shirts and stockings, slicing bread, chopping onions and garlic, putting in the key and turning the knob—a thousand daily movements come rushing to mind while Angie takes the margarine out of the fridge. She's got on a Frida Kahlo T-shirt and silver-plated earrings. An enormous Gaugin print decorates the wall. She has fabulous taste. Her eye flourishes in the humblest corners, like the bathroom sink where discs of scented soap give off lemon and rose under water.

I think of the words "bad hand," "bad arm." What is "bad" about it is the opposite of what the good can do: cook, sew, touch, dress. Imagine walking home alone in the dark from the train station knowing that if an assailant approaches, you have only one arm with which to defend yourself. Imagine further that you are a black woman in your fifties in a city with one of the highest per capita murder rates in the nation. The disability is significant in that it forces the development of her entire relationship with the "abled" world.

Because Angie cannot sew now and because she cannot paint, she writes. She has taped on her refrigerator two poems by Lucille Clifton, a black woman, a poet, a mother. One is "What the mirror said":

listen,
you a wonder,
you a city of a woman.
you got a geography
of your own.
listen,
somebody need a map
to understand you.
somebody need directions
to move around you.
listen,
woman,
you not a noplace
anonymous
girl;
mister with his hands on you
he got his hands
on some
damn
b o d y!

This poem speaks of affirming the body and all its history. The body is a metaphor for a life; trace a scar, there is a story. Part of the reason Angie responds so strongly to Clifton's work is that a good number of her own poems originate in a dialogue with her body. In the writing workshop, she frequently uses her hair or arm or skin as metaphor for a range of emotions; she *begins* by looking at herself through the mirror of corporal associations. Her bad arm rests on her thigh, and she asks its history, what it can and cannot do. She asks the body what it remembers and what it has lost in her own poem "Picking up the pieces." Here is one part:

I started to lose body parts
        a limb here   a graft there
        at the surgeon's hand
and by the time of the fifth decade plus

. . . lots of scars that look like lightning
bolts—in strategic places—I don't think of myself
as covered with excess baggage—
it's all simply God's handiwork, and that's me
Cause that's what I am—
Her handiwork indeed—

Angie's poetic development moves in the direction of refining images, placing her words more specifically and courageously on the point of her woman's history. The more accurately she defines in words the parts of the body, the deeper her commitment to language becomes.

IN HER MEMOIR, Angie examines the history of her body, beginning with her pregnancy at age sixteen. Her pregnancy effected profound changes; though the child she delivered did not live, she chose to remain married. Angie dropped out of high school and, with no diploma or significant job skills, moved in with her husband and his family. These changes strained the relationship with her mother, cutting her adrift from the support of her primary family "both emotionally and physically." Her own mother had married young as a result of pregnancy. Angie believes that she was a painful and physical reincarnation of her mother's own life, a "living reminder of some painful memories" better pushed away than examined.

After her parents separated, home to Angie was her mother and brother. The psychological and financial rift between Angie and her mother represents the loss of a primary network of care and support. Many homeless women have lost, or never really experienced, a home environment that intervenes with the street, so when they have a financial or psychological crisis, a good number of them have no place to turn. This fundamental tear sets individuals adrift, usually at the worst time. Psychological or physical emergencies often rupture already delicate relations, and the woman who becomes homeless often is the refugee from such a crisis.

Many of the women I've met over the last two years began their homeless experience in their teenage years. Frequently, a young woman will run away from an abusive parent or caretaker, taking with her only limited systems of support and precious little but energy and ingenuity to keep body and soul together. Those who stay on the streets, in squats, or exploitative living situations with adults fashion a safety net that is fraught with danger; usually, these desperate attempts to find a better life further isolate the person in crisis. Options get fewer and fewer.

At sixteen, Angie chose to marry the father of her first child. Part of the reason for her decision, I suspect, was that in this time of indecision and profound change, she needed the support her mother could not give. The subtle, multi-layered exchanges that define human interaction satisfy beyond speech; the loss of these can, conversely, collapse desire into despair. The painful distance Angie felt from her mother spurred her past doubt—should I stay married?—into marriage. In that transfer, Angie lost her mother. "When my mother died," Angie once remarked to me, "I felt I had already gone through much of the grieving process."

This break from her mother sounded deep into the young girl. While Angie stayed married, many women in comparable situations have no place to go and nowhere to turn. The roots of homelessness reach far back, tangling economic and vocational realities, making the landscape of shelter and sustenance multidimensional. Angie has been, in her own words, "blessed" with a persistent courage to fight for a good life for herself and her children. She relentlessly sought healing that would connect her inner life to her outer. This insistence is what shapes her journey and is the fuel for her determination to have a whole, lucky life.

The birth of her second child, the older of her two boys, especially renewed her faith and strength. If her body catalogued grief at the loss of the first-born girl, it rejoiced in the natural delivery of her son. Angie chooses a physical event, motherhood, to evidence the recovery of her confidence as a woman. She says:

> I think childbirth toughens a woman in some spiritual, unseen way. It did me. I felt that if I could survive *that* experience, then I could survive anything. That feeling of confidence was

something that was in my life for a long time. It was like something wonderful inside that was quietly kept.

The birth of this son without the assistance of medical staff or drugs became for Angie the event to which she could return again and again as an icon of survival and pride. It is something within herself, a capability of the body, that was a secret, "quietly kept." It is something that could not be taken away.

Why this phrasing? Why locate this courage and confidence in the body? Why choose this event above all others?

When Angie was a young girl, she was sexually abused by an older teenage stepcousin. In putting her autobiography together, she fought the desire to keep the assault out of the text. It is difficult to write in a way that conveys a painful experience without trivializing or diminishing it. Words can seem insubstantial, inadequate to the task. Survivors of trauma tread that darkness between private terror, the words that name it, and the world to which it is spoken. War veterans and survivors of rape, assault, and other forms of violence learn to be suspicious of words because of their experience with inadequate legal procedures that often further compound the victimization. These survivors often have their words turned around by the victimizers—"you asked for it," "it's for your own good"; or they find that words simply cannot represent the depth and scope of what they have endured.

Because Angie was assaulted as a child and because silence surrounded the abuse, it burrowed deep into a private, secret place. That trauma triggered disordered attempts to process the damage, but in the mind and body of this young girl, she simultaneously cried out and kept quiet, none of it happening at a conscious level. Her body was the story she sought to tell, but could not.

The confidence, then, the thing kept quietly inside, which toughens her in some spiritual way, a toughness not exactly rational or apprehended through logic, was her quiet declaration of survival. That it happened privately, in the body, only much later to be brought into words, illuminates the vital pathway from which

Angie writes: a union of the sensual and the textual pressing on towards healing.

Angie acknowledges that the historical experience of black women in America is one in which the body was enslaved. She muses about a possible correlation between the rage and frustration of being a black woman in this nation with its bitter racial history and the addiction to food:

> I've been doing some thinking about the statistics I've seen recently that state that almost 50 percent of black women are overweight. And I wonder a lot about what that's all about. I think it has something to do with the stress of having to cope in a racist world.

While she does not spend much time on this subject in her memoir, it's important to see Angie's relationship to the larger community of black people. She consciously challenges legacies of racism in this nation by putting herself into words. Before Emancipation, slaves were forbidden to read or write, so a marker of freedom was literacy. Slave narratives—some written by the former slave, some recorded through interviews—were among the earliest African-American texts: putting experience into words was resistance, and the deep investment in authenticating experience through writing one's own story is a tradition much valued in black literature. Writing was a way, too, of staking a claim on existence as a thinking, complete being in the new homeland.

In her own reflections on autobiography in *Talking Back: Thinking Feminist, Thinking Black*, writer and scholar bell hooks explains that she was seeking to write her life story into a public discourse that has poorly and inadequately represented black women. She emphasizes that working-class black women in particular have had their lives obscured through inaccurate representation by others or by a silence just as effective. Angie's voice speaks against the silencing that poverty wields, as well as the brackets around "freedoms" for a black woman born before the passage of the Civil Rights Act.

THROUGHOUT HER LIFE, Angie has struggled to keep her body whole while it seemed to be flying apart at the seams. Parallel to the body, Angie faced increasing mental pressure. Her mind broke off in periodic hallucinations and delusions. She learned to recognize the symptoms of a breakdown and would check into clinics or mental health facilities to prevent danger to herself or others. Diagnoses and medications varied from episode to episode, none of which lessened the increased alienation mental illness was effecting.

Thousands of poor and homeless woman are mentally ill. Inadequate treatment coupled with the chaos of living without shelter keeps many women isolated in the revolving door of crisis mental health management. Federal monies have been reduced, of course, forcing individuals with no support system out onto the streets. Very often, those with debilitating psychological disorders slip beyond the reach of family and friends *because of* their illness. The behavioral impact of the illness alienates family and friends in any number of ways, mixing shame, confusion, and frustration into the rejection of the person who suffers the illness.

Angie describes the unseen wall of manic-depression as a kind of torture: the internal voices compel a world of ill vision and sound at desperate odds with the outside world. The erosion of a healing community, if it existed at all, is gradual, shaking the member into an even more realized alienation. Worst of all, the person most in need of help frequently cannot recognize it.

Angie believes that the primary reason she was able to avoid more protracted and debilitating homelessness was because she asked for help. Whether the break was mental, physical, or financial, she worked within the system to get help. Independent and proud by nature, she knew that to save a life for her sons and for herself, she would have to navigate the labyrinthine bureaucracy of social services. Her persistence led to an outpatient therapist in 1992, at which time her illness was correctly diagnosed. She is all too aware that many women and men were not so "blessed," remaining trapped behind those walls in need of a more sustained, consistent care.

Employing, self-consciously, a vocabulary of therapy and healing, Angie devises a narrative that creatively mirrors her near-lifelong search for repair. She hopes her story will reach other women in similar circumstances who, by reading about her healing, will be able to imagine their own. Angie's story is also an act of resistance to the sort of silence that cloaks mental and physical illness in a choking net around those who suffer. Writing is surviving—in her words, "a very important part of the ongoing process of healing and reconnecting with the whole and creative female I . . . was at the outset." Her autobiography is both agent and witness to that belief.

Conclusions

EIGHT

"WHERE WRITING COMES IN": A DIALOGUE

*Near the end of the process of developing this book, Debbie
and Jeanie sat down for a concluding talk.*

DEBBIE: Sponsors of our programs or readers of this book might be
surprised by the level of excitement the women we worked with felt
in coming to a poem or story. Some may think that the women
wouldn't be able to analyze literature or they wouldn't be able to
understand it, but they did because they let themselves, intuitively,
without preconceptions that said they couldn't. At Rachael's House,
I found I could bring in any author from an African-American poet
to Gabriel Garcia Marquez to the Ancient Greeks, and the women
loved it all. One of the best times we had was when I introduced
them to Aristophanes' *Lysistrata*. Here's this Greek play from 411
B.C. about how the women of Athens joined forces with the
women of Sparta to stop the war that had been raging for decades
by withholding sex from their men until they made peace. Ann
played Lysistrata, I played the commissioner, Georgia played
several of the Spartan women's parts, and other women read
the male and female chorus parts in unison. It was a blast. They
loved it—partly because it is a hilarious play and partly because
the battle of the sexes was raging then in the same ways as now.
The women were fascinated with the play: it was creative and
new to them, yet reading it established connections with circumstances, values, and decisions throughout history. It took us
three or four classes to read the whole thing, and every day more

women would come because they had heard we were doing this great play.

JEANIE: I had that experience too. There wasn't one genre, one poet, one fiction writer whom someone in the class didn't appreciate. And we used material from the Psalms to Holocaust poets to hard-hitting Michelle T. Clinton, from spoken word poetry to Anne Sexton to academic poets like T. S. Eliot for whom you have to have a certain amount of background to understand their work. In fact, some of the women wanted the class to be more academic: they wanted you to be teacher and them to have pens, paper, and pads and for the session to function like a class. For many who were high school dropouts, the classes repaired a break they had with school. Even for those who graduated, these workshops helped reconnect them with their intellectual lives which had been vivid and flourishing before everything snapped and got translated into a different language. In Angie's case, the snap was caused by mental illness; in Gayle's, addiction; and for both of them, bad childhood experiences.

DEBBIE: But I also found working with the women reminded me of how many university students used to tell me, "Aw, gosh, we have to take composition. We have to take this literature. I have an English-teacher phobia!" In high school, they would read these poems and stories and just regurgitate what they were told was the meaning. College students I've taught have somehow been conditioned so they don't know how to come to literature for all the good things: what they can discover in it about themselves, about the writer, about their own culture, or how they fit in all the stories that are around us. The women in our workshops also generally had this notion that there shouldn't be an excitement when you read a poem—so finding excitement in our classes was totally unexpected for them.

JEANIE: And when they had more of a vocabulary, when they started to want words like "metaphor" and "image" and "character," those words became tools, not things to be afraid of anymore.

DEBBIE: When we were teaching in jail and you and I came to the readings with very different approaches, it was exciting and liberating for the women to see the differences between us and realize how many interpretations were possible. There especially, we had entered into a space where language had been dismissed as having no importance whatsoever. How much did we have to work as teachers just to give the women a sense that they had the right to speak their own feelings? And then they had to find the language to do it on paper.

JEANIE: That begins to get at the difference between telling and writing a story, because I maintain that writing is finding things: it is a process of exploration, not just a matter of reporting what you already know. Look at how many times we've been in classes and people have started off writing about a favorite shirt and ended up writing about their grandmother's kindness to them when they were five. These associations just travel. Something about writing gets you to a different place: it accomplishes something. In a writing workshop, everyone's just talk-talk-talk at first; then, we do our honoring ritual and the pace of the class slows down a bit, but there are still all the personalities jumping and connecting; then, we do a reading or introduce the theme for the day; and then, this group dialogue shifts onto the page and everyone sits there for half an hour writing. After the writing, the class becomes more respectful of each person's voice. Suddenly the woman you were annoyed with because she came in late dragging her bags and disrupting class is a woman with a voice too. And everyone leaves the class feeling a little more human, more dignified, and more valued than they were before.

DEBBIE: Georgia and the other women at Rachael's said the same thing. That place and time for writing were important to them, and they didn't let anyone violate it. Although it did take a long time to get them to trust, in the end they realized it wasn't me doing it—it was them doing it. The most important part of that whole process was that after everyone stopped writing, whether they had written one paragraph or two pages, each person would read to the group what she had written, and with that each one received a profound respect that she seldom received anywhere else. Each person listened quietly. They nodded their heads. They listened to every word. They *applauded* after each woman read. That stunned me the first time, but you could feel the energy going up in the room. Maybe some people would think reading out loud was a waste of time, but that was the most essential part of the process: they thought it, wrote it, and then said it. With that, they had been appreciated by a community of other writers. I will never believe anything in my heart more than I believe that these women will carry what happened in those classes with them. Always.

JEANIE: That makes me think of this woman who comes to class at the dinner program. She's mentally ill, a substance abuser, and a prostitute; she lives in a room in one of those single-occupancy buildings. She wrote once with such insistence and intensity about a jar of instant coffee on her nightstand. At first, I didn't understand the image. It seemed dissociated from anything else going on in the poem, and she kept going back to it. I learned slowly that this jar of coffee somehow represented her landlord, who rapes her. I guess he feels she's a hooker anyway, her body doesn't matter, so it's part of the rental agreement. So one night she came in to our classroom at the dinner program. No one else was there, and we sat together on the couch. She was going on about what had happened over the last week or so, very companionable and mellow, and she put her hand on my back. It was a physical contact she initiated: she wanted a hug. "You're the only person," she said, "who listens to me. You're the only person who asks me what I think. You're the only person who asks me what I feel." When you're a prostitute, living in poverty, and mentally ill, and you know as a woman your value has plummeted to the point that rape and rent, rape and currency, are almost the same thing, then of course nobody's asking what your experience is. The impact the class has had on this woman is enormous. And sometimes when I forget that these women—my students—are homeless, that touch on the back and her saying "you're the only person who listens" reminds me of the distance between their lives and mine, and how that small place where we connected helps them to reclaim their dignity as individuals.

DEBBIE: I remember being surprised that we had a hard time getting the women to write about homelessness. I thought at first it was that we had just started and we weren't accepted yet. Maybe they saw us like all the other volunteers or social workers, always someone prying into your life; and here we were asking them to just lay it out. But even after they discovered we were not going to label or judge them, very few of them wanted to write about homelessness. I think they saw it as a part of their story, but it wasn't who they were. In class, they finally found a place where they could be who they were.

JEANIE: Did you ever ask yourself, of all the women we worked with, why did we connect in particular with the ones we included in this book?

DEBBIE: When I first read Georgia's writing, she brought me all these pages in pencil, none of the t's crossed; at first, I was just trying to read it, but then, I started really connecting with her reverence for the past and feeling of loss for a time that was close and intimate, when life was different from the way it is now. I was sincerely moved by Ann both because of her images and because she was such a creative person. The initial connection with Dionne came about when we did our first class at the jail and I read journal entries about my friend dying with AIDS. Two or three months later, she told me she was HIV-positive. With all of them, something clicked, you know, to make these particular women trust us enough and to be so enthusiastic about this book.

JEANIE: I think it's partly because we took them seriously. And part of the reason that the connection was so serious was that we had an investment in it too. I can't remember exactly what happened with me in the beginning. It just happened little bit by little bit. One person would let me in, and then because I knew one person around the writing table, the other people would be just this much more willing to let me in a teeny-weeny little bit. That's where longevity has a lot to do with it. Trust isn't something you can just step into; it's something you have to earn. I'll never forget after the reading at the dinner program, Dorothy (one woman who'd been part of it) had done a fabulous job; she was dressed up in this gorgeous dress, her hair all done. After the whole thing was over and the vans were coming to pick the women up to take them to the trailers and shelters, Dorothy hugged me and said, "Well, when will we see you again?" I realized that she thought this was it: that the event meant the end of our relationship because that had been her history. Usually, people just come and throw these feel-good events, and then they leave.

But these strong connections that we formed can also be scary. One night Gayle called me before she went back into rehab. She was talking a mile a minute about the book and what was going on in her life and I was a little afraid that she was depending on me too much. You know, Gayle's life is so different from mine, yet it's not an artificial connection between us. It's a deep, soul connection which is so unwieldy and incongruous. People I know who don't have any association with homeless people usually can't imagine being friends with a homeless person: they think we couldn't possibly have anything in common on which to form a relationship. But this book is evidence that we can have those connections. There is something essential in the dialogue that writing provides. It's a linkage that doesn't exist in our culture very often.

DEBBIE: I agree. When the television people came to Rachael's, what upset me was that they kept pointing to writing as therapy in some abstract way. But for many of the women, I was a part of their lives. Writing about their lives may have been a form of therapy for them, but it went way beyond that—it goes to the connections between people. These women were not simply objects of analysis for me; they were my friends. I would go home and I would worry about them. What are they going to do? How are they going to get up and get out of here? How are they going to believe in themselves? How can they see creativity as a way to get out of this situation? And I felt so helpless sometimes and sad and depressed over the whole thing. I had to try to keep some distance because I never came to this program to save anyone. These women write about the hard knocks of life, but all of us have had the hard knocks of life in different manifestations. The important thing is that when we get our stories together like some big ole fabric, we're *all* enriched by it. Not only in the writing of it, but the reading of it.

JEANIE: When I was writing about Gayle's and Angie's chapters, I kept thinking that I wanted the reader to know the women I know and see what I see. I kept asking myself should I talk about this funny thing they did or this profound thing they said or this gesture that was unbelievably kind or this funny irreverence.

DEBBIE: When I started thinking about this book, it was sort of a political thing—that these women were voiceless and people needed to hear what they said. But then, as I started reading their writing, I started thinking, well, these are human stories just like everybody else's. And however we solve that dilemma of who makes it or how someone becomes homeless and how they function in that world are just human stories and I cared less about that political part of it.

JEANIE: But telling these human stories *is* a political act. It's not political in the sense of walking up to the White House or Capitol Hill saying, "Put three million dollars as opposed to two million into homeless programs." But these women's voices have been silenced and marginalized, and the violence that plays on their lives becomes internalized. So by writing—articulating their thoughts and transferring them from the private to the public sphere— they're affirming themselves as full citizens.

DEBBIE: I remember how awkward it was at the open house at Rachael's. It's sort of funny now. Here I am, the grand master of ceremonies, and Georgia's reading and Minnie's reading. Michelle was going to read, but she freaked and didn't. Eleanor read, and Ann sang a song. And I'm looking out at these visitors at the open house. Some of them are from the neighborhood, but most of them are white and in three-piece suits and dressed up. As I was introducing someone, I looked through the mass of dressed-up white people, and leaning on the radiator in the hall was Violet. And I'm thinking, what's Violet thinking about? Then I saw Thomasina and I thought, what's Thomasina thinking about? Then Deborah. What's Deborah thinking about? And I felt so awkward. I felt that we were putting on a contrived show like vaudeville or something. But after it was over, when everyone came up and talked with the writers, it was a tremendous boost to their own witnessing of themselves and their right to speak that people were interested, really interested in what they said. Nobody was interested in what they said on a day-to-day basis.

JEANIE: Do you think homeless people will read this book?

DEBBIE: Yes, I really do. Before I started WritersCorps, I would have said no. But after the experience with the anthology at Rachael's, absolutely. They may not read your and my chapters! But they will read the women's chapters. I know they will. And I wonder what they'll think.

JEANIE: Well, when I gave Gayle the edited version of her chapter, she right away shared it with this friend of hers who is in a similar situation. The woman came up to me and she said all excited, "This is so good. It's really good." Gayle will be able to reach people that my chapters will never touch. My dream about this book from the beginning is that homeless people will read it. And that, more important, Gayle, Georgia, Angie, Dionne, and Ann can say, "See, we did it." However, in my own writing, sometimes I felt a little like I was objectifying the women through analysis.

DEBBIE: I was concerned about that too, but what I love about this book is that people will get to read these women's own texts. We may have helped them organize pieces of their writing or encouraged them to expand on certain points and we certainly provided the support for them to write what they did, but we have not written it *for* them in any way. These are their own stories about their own lives. Some people write books about the homeless that are nothing but treatises of exploitation because they don't let the individual person's voice be heard. And then I've read some that say that they've made a composite of several people, and I just want to scream. Here, readers are free to make their own judgments, draw their own conclusions, find their own enjoyment, whatever they want to get from the women's chapters and from ours.

JEANIE: I recently read *Dreaming: Hard Luck and Good Times in America* by Carolyn See. It's her life story, and she talks about her addiction, her abuses, bad marriages, and other screw-ups. But she always had writing to express herself—this dialogue that kept her from being so isolated. And in that way, I could see connections between her story and the stories of the women in this book. But then I thought, well, Carolyn See was in a social sphere in which being a hard drinker was what everybody was doing and so she was still accepted by society. It wasn't like being a hard drinker as well as a prostitute and black and poor. I just had the sense that when Carolyn See was making little steps to get away from screwing up, there was a place to go, a network that didn't further stigmatize her. Whereas for Dionne, her biggest network was in prison. Big favor that does for your social life and your resume.

DEBBIE: You know, I asked Dionne to give me some stuff for a resume because when she got out of jail, she had to get her own job, and she had no one else to help her with this. But she didn't give me anything, and finally I asked her why, and she says, "What am I gonna put on there? That I was a bartender and a go-go dancer?" She had already given up at that point. But, you know, I also shared with Dionne my own frustrations about my career and my life. We didn't come to the women with ideas about being perfect. And we admitted we weren't perfect ourselves in our own writings that we did in class and read aloud. That's another reason for the connection with the women: we all opened up our human foibles for inspection.

JEANIE: Sometimes we were walking foibles. I'll never forget my first time at Rachael's after you left this incredible legacy of writing workshops. It was a hundred degrees and I got off at the metro stop and am walking over there with my Persian rug of hair piled on my head. I'm sweating and I have four thousand papers stuffed in my bag and I don't know where I'm going. I get there and walk in and there's this big fan there, big as Frankenstein, and it just so happens that my exercise for that day involved all these pieces of little papers with things like your first kiss, the secret you never told your parents. All these women had just eaten lunch and they're napping because it's so hot and their necks are just falling, while the ones who are awake are watching me slosh around in a pouring sweat chasing after these little pieces of paper that the fan was blowing around. Here I was trying to hold it together and create a cohesive class experience, and I felt like such a clown.

DEBBIE: I think my worst class at Rachael's was one day I got this bright idea to combine two exercises. So I took my drum and I'm gonna do this mystical thing. I talked about what it means to think about one's purpose in life and then what it means to write it. Then, I got them to write what they thought their purpose in life was, and I sealed it in an envelope and said, in a few months, I'll give these back to you and you can see if your life has been working in the direction of your purpose. Then, I had them write down some awful thing they wanted to get rid of in their lives and they crumbled up that piece of paper. I put a hat in the middle of the living room, and I started beating the drum like I had done for a Sufi thing once. Well, I'm beating the drum, beating the drum, and they're walking around in a circle. Everybody's walking and walking, I'm waiting for the energy, you know, and then they start moaning, "How long we gotta walk?" Then, the circle became an oval because there wasn't enough room there. They're walking and walking, and people are coming in the front door saying, "What they doing?" Walking and beating, walking and beating, and then I had them throw their dark secrets in the hat and we took them outside and burned them. And the women were like—so what? I was so embarrassed.

JEANIE: Yeah, but look at the successes. Gloria, another woman at the dinner program, is a perfect example. She gave me her whole portfolio once, and it had these amazing comics of homeless people in dumpsters. In it she wrote mostly about being assaulted, but there's this one beautiful passage about sitting in a park. She spends a lot of time in the park, looking at the birds and trees, and having this complete, beautiful, and peaceable experience with nature. I'm sure she'd rather have this communion with her children, lovers, or friends, but she can't. And so she has it with nature and with her painting and writing. She's an example of a person who finds incredible power and sustenance and life in telling her story to herself and in painting a world. I don't want to minimize the pain she has, but at the same time there is a beauty she has found that is priceless.

DEBBIE: Were you surprised at that? Were you surprised when you first started the program that you would find people who used creativity to make their lives better?

JEANIE: I think I was. The chaos and lack of privacy in their lives is incredible, and the world just sees Gloria as some homeless, batty woman wearing a gold hat with a feather sticking out. But the fact that she made the choice to be a loving person, not a bitter, angry person, and to create art and communion with nature is a courage that I'm sure I wouldn't be capable of. She calls herself an artist; our connection was that she would always say "artists like us." Once, she wrote this really amazing piece about taking care of a baby girl who had been violated. She wrote about it so beautifully, with so much compassion. And she read with no shame and complete confidence that everyone in the group would see and feel what she was feeling. For her—among artists—she felt that we were a special community where normal rules didn't hold and where you could share these things because we respected speaking about them. When she read her work that day, everyone was crying and sharing their stories and reading their stuff. I had to take another woman out of the room. She doesn't read or write, classified as retarded, an orphan, raped by her brother, and just all this awful stuff. She was crying and talking, and I just wrote down all she said and it was really, really hard. Then, at the end, Gloria led us all in prayer, everyone holding hands, and we were all just praying for all the pain and survival from pain. It was an incredible experience. All the women were sharing it, but it really represented this woman's induction into the class.

DEBBIE: That reminds me of the honoring ritual we did. It's such a wonderful way of making you look for things in people and events that you respect. But even more than that, in writing, it develops awareness. It makes you reflect back on the day or the week, so that those little things that might have escaped you are given special awareness. That's what we always tried to do in writing—help people be aware of the little details because they suggest so much about the overall fabric of life.

JEANIE: It also reinforces the need for a close community. I really think that people need to have a sense of belonging and a sense that people care what they do, that their actions have ramifications that matter. The honoring makes you aware of that and of being in a community where people are open and trusting, so that if you violate this trust, you detonate something in that group. Having an investment in a community like that is opposite to living in a callous environment that doesn't care whether or not you make it. It seems to me that America is so focused on the individual making it, making it, making it, that when you screw up, it's your screw-up. Nobody else's. But the truth is that we *don't* function in a void. The reason I'm not homeless even though I've lived on the edge so much is because my family won't let me slip.

DEBBIE: I asked one of the women who works at Rachael's about that one day. I said that I couldn't understand how these women can be homeless and their folks never try to do anything for them. They've just left them out here. They don't seem to care anything for them. She said that the ones who are addicts have probably stolen, ripped everybody off; the ones who are mentally ill have probably done similar things to alienate them; and the others, their families are probably poorer than they are and they can't help them. But you know, I find that hard to believe. Hard to believe.

JEANIE: Just think of cultures that are poorer than the average American family, but they provide.

DEBBIE: Right. And what they provide more than food or money or housing is the feeling that you are part of a community. Maybe this is the core of it: that when you feel like you're a part of a community, you owe that community something, and that something is accountability for your actions. If you take care of me, I have to live by a certain code that is not destructive to the community. But people have to feel loved, respected, and a part before they can follow those community rules. You see all these people who are just cast away, wandering by themselves. I'm remembering that gangster woman in our first class at jail. When she wrote her story, I remember you and I both were stunned. Her story was: one day my homeboy and I were walking down the street, and somebody rode by and shot him, and I stepped over him and I went home. No emotion whatsoever. And you know at that point I'm some stupid, overzealous writing teacher and I asked her how she felt about that. And she said she didn't feel anything. She just sneered at me and gave me this face. She was so young, and she felt nothing. It was a complete dehumanization. And it's not just her, you know; the finger points at all of us.

JEANIE: Well, I feel good that you and I have helped a few women move toward a happy ending—or more accurately, a happy new beginning. I noticed recently in *Poets & Writers* magazine a call for submissions from writers with disabilities. Before this project, Angie would have never considered herself enough of a writer to submit something. But now she will. Now, she thinks of herself as a writer and she looks to improve herself as a writer. This book is something she can give to her grandkids; she's really proud to have accomplished this. She can apply for a job in a bookstore and say she has a book on the shelf. For the women, this book is a tool they can use to help themselves; it's something they didn't have a year ago.

DEBBIE: One of the main things I want from this book is for people to see these five individuals as people who deserve a chance.

JEANIE: And to accept them as they are. Their lives are different and that difference should not be minimized, yet people often seem to fear difference because they've been taught that diversity can alienate. But in our programs, we had a constant joy in discovering who we all were. It's individuals who make leaps into the enormous cultural abysses of race and gender and social class and make connections. It's individuals who have to have the courage and the faith to believe that people can make these leaps and, once you make one or two or three, then when that next opportunity opens, you can walk right through that door and not stand on the peripheries.

DEBBIE: We're not so naive as to think that writing alone can open all the doors, you know, because it won't. But although it won't break down all the realities of racism or poverty, it can contribute to that breaking—even if it's just a little crack.

Writing, I think, helps you realize that you are more than all the stories that have been told about you. It helps you realize that there are many doors, many outlets that are creative and positive. If you knock on one door and it won't open to you, you have the faith to go on to the next one. And the next one. And the next one until it opens. You need a firm center, a real connection to who you are, to be able to do that. And that's where writing comes in. Along with community. And most of all, courage.

SUGGESTIONS FOR FURTHER READING

Angelou, Maya. *I Know Why the Caged Bird Sings*. New York: Bantam, 1993. Reprint of 1969 edition.

This ground-breaking memoir of an African-American woman's childhood through young adulthood is a classic and a model everywhere for the gritty portrayal of an extraordinary ordinary life, presented in a deeply nuanced narrative voice. Recommended by Jeanie.

Aptheker, Bettina. *Tapestries of Life: Women's Work, Women's Consciousness, and the Meaning of Daily Experience*. Amherst: Univ. of Massachusetts Press, 1989.

This book examines women's culture by placing women in the center of the discourse about gender, race, and class. The author draws upon a variety of sources—women writers, poets, artists, dancers, musicians, academics, factory workers, and laborers—to create women's cultural heritage as the foundation for changing contemporary women's consciousness of themselves. Recommended by Debbie.

Aristotle, *Poetics*. Richard Janko, trans. Indianapolis: Hackett Publishing, 1987.

Aristotle's investigation of the effects of poetry and drama is worth reading for anyone interested in writing as emotional cathar-sis. It is also useful for any writer who is interested in how ideas fil-ter through history. Recommended by Debbie.

Bard, Marjorie. *Organizational and Community Responses to Domes-tic Abuse and Homelessness.* New York: Garland Publishing, 1994.
Written by a woman who experienced homelessness, this is a fiercely independent text about the stories women tell themselves (she calls it "idionarrating") and what they show her. Great reading, as well as a sort of informal study of various ways in which women live homeless in this country. Recommended by Jeanie.

Behn, Robin, and Chase Twichell, eds. *The Practice of Poetry.* New York: Harper Perennial, 1992.
An excellent sourcebook for writing exercise ideas. Recom-mended by Debbie.

Clifton, Lucille. *good woman: poems and a memoir, 1969–1980.* New York: BOA Editions, 1987.
This book of poems and narrative shines with uncanny detail, magic, and history of the life of one black woman speaking great truths to all women and all people. A good model and inspiration for creative writing exercises. Recommended by Jeanie.

Des Pres, Terrence. *Writing into the World: Essays, 1973–1987.* New York: Viking, 1991.
A thought-provoking exploration of ideas about the relationship between the writing life and conscious political inquiry. Recom-mended by Jeanie.

Duarte, Carlota. *Odella: A Hidden Survivor.* Albuquerque: Univ. of New Mexico Press, 1990.
An original, striking collaboration between a homeless woman and a photographic artist. Recommended by Jeanie.

Felski, Rita. *Beyond Feminist Aesthetics: Feminist Literature and Social Change.* Cambridge: Harvard Univ. Press, 1989.

Felski examines two forms of women's writing—the confessional and the novel of self-discovery. Of particular note is her attempt to construct a critical basis for examining women's writing within its historical and social context. She touches also on women's differences such as race, class, and sexual orientation, but does not go far enough in my opinion. However, her suggestion of forming a "feminist counter-public sphere" in which social change is possible is written without jargon and is thought-provoking in its bold call to action. Recommended by Debbie.

Golden, Marita, and Susan Richards Shreve, eds. *Skin Deep: Black Women and White Women Write About Race.* New York: Doubleday, 1995.

A diverse and well-written source for dialogue about race between black and white women. Recommended by Jeanie.

Grudin, Robert. *The Grace of Great Things: Creativity and Innovation.* New York: Ticknor and Fields, 1990.

An insightful meditation on the social aspects of creativity, innovation, and imagination. Recommended by Debbie.

Heilbrun, Carolyn G. *Writing a Woman's Life.* New York: Ballantine, 1988.

An excellent book on the influences of social convention and a patriarchal structure on the shaping and content of women's autobiographical writing. Recommended by Debbie.

hooks, bell. *Feminist Theory: From Margin to Center.* Boston: South End Press, 1984.

hooks, bell. *Talking Back: Thinking Feminist, Thinking Black.* Boston: South End Press, 1989.

These two collections of essays have helped me nearly every step of the way, in my life and my work. They articulate difficult issues with courage. Further, through example and form, they set a standard for feminist inquiry that does not shy away from intra-feminist challenges, including race, sexual preference, and class. Recommended by Jeanie.

Hughes, Elaine Farris. *Writing from the Inner Self.* New York: HarperCollins, 1991.
This book combines meditation and writing exercises to free imagination and creativity. Recommended by Debbie.

Karr, Mary. *The Liar's Club.* New York: Viking, 1995.
This memoir is gorgeous, unflinching, and soaked in geography. One of the best memoirs, hands-down, I have ever read. Recommended by Jeanie.

Kaufman, Gershen, and L. Raphael. *Coming Out of Shame.* New York: Doubleday, 1996.
This insightful book examines connections between the effects of shame and personal silencing. For the most part, the focus is on gay men and lesbians; however, the discussion is useful for understanding how any marginalized person who grows up among negative stories and stereotypes internalizes shame. Recommended by Debbie.

Kotre, John. *White Gloves: How We Create Ourselves Through Memory.* New York: Free Press, 1995.
An excellent introduction to theories of memory, including memory-librarian, memory-mythmaker, and memory hierarchy. Recommended by Debbie.

Kowit, Steve. *In the Palm of Your Hand: The Poet's Portable Workshop.* Gardiner, Maine: Tilbury House, 1995.
A wonderful collection of poems, readings, and exercises designed for a group or an individual on his or her own. A terrific resource for exercises you can immediately employ or adapt as needed. Recommended by Jeanie.

Lorde, Audre. *Sister Outsider.* Trumansburg, NY: Crossing Press, 1984.
Lorde's essays and speeches in this collection are particularly poignant, insightful, and relevant for women writers. My favorites are these essays: "Poetry Is Not a Luxury," "The Transformation of Silence into Language and Action," "Uses of the Erotic," and "The Master's Tools Will Never Dismantle the Master's House." Recommended by Debbie.

Olney, James. *Metaphors of Self.* Princeton: Princeton Univ. Press, 1972.
Olney's introduction is particularly instructive in discussing how the form of autobiography is a definition of the writer's self at a particular time and place and how style and construction in autobiography are indicative of the writer's creative consciousness. Recommended by Debbie.

Randall, William Lowell. *The Stories We Are: An Essay on Self-Creation.* Toronto: Univ. of Toronto Press, 1995.
An inclusive, well-researched book on the poetics of autobiography. Recommended by Debbie.

Smith, Barbara, ed. *Home Girls: A Black Feminist Anthology.* New York: Kitchen Table/Women of Color Press, 1983.
This collection of literary works is an excellent starting point for anyone interested in African-American women writers and the struggles that accompany creating a life in writing. Smith's introduction provides a critical perspective on the relationship among feminism, writing, and African-American women. Recommended by Debbie.

Walker, Alice. *In Search of Our Mothers' Gardens.* New York: Harcourt Brace Jovanovich, 1983.
A classic work for any woman's library. The personal and political nature of the essays makes them excellent for discussion topics and writing exercises. Recommended by Debbie.

INDEX

ACKNOWLEDGMENTS

So many people supported us along the way, but we would like to offer special acknowledgment to our team teacher, Imani Tolliver, for her sisterhood, faith, and commitment. We thank Willa Morris and the staff at Rachael's House, Linda Kaufman and the staff at the Dinner Program for Homeless Women, Norma Jennings and the staff at the D.C. Correctional Treatment Facility, and Kenneth Carroll, Diem Jones, and all the members of WritersCorps. We thank Carolyn Forché for her unabated belief in WritersCorps, and we would like to recognize Marita Golden, Brother Ba, and Margaret for special assistance. Also we thank AmeriCorps and the National Endowment for the Arts for providing the funding. In developing this book, we thank Donna Jonté and Tyra Lindquist for their helpful suggestions, and we especially thank our publisher, Lynn Page Whittaker, for her commitment to all the writers in this book and her belief and support in making voices and stories such as these part of a more public discourse. Finally, we thank all the women who participated in classes and joined our writing community.

—Deborah Pugh and Jeanie Tietjen

Many voices make up that one we call our own. For all their whispers and shouts, I'd like to thank my mother, Martha, who walks in my footsteps every day; my sister, Kim, who always surprises me with her courage and unconditional love; my niece, Lakin, who is as apt to open my eyes as shut my mouth; mi Fortuna de Amor, Issy, who offers me a vision that nourishes my soul and makes my heart dance a wild tango; and Bledsoe and Eslie, my grandparents. Last, I thank Jeanie for her dervish energy, her limitless supply of generosity, and her fierce dedication to the smallest motes of joy.

—*Deborah Pugh*

Profound gratitude and love to the whole Tietjen clan, for their enduring faith, support, and belief in the essential good thing, especially to my father for developing in me a respect for the power of right words and actions. Also to the Westberg-Beggs clan for your many years of shelter, vision, and affection. And to Dana Levin, a poet and a sister.

—*Jeanie Tietjen*

DEBORAH PUGH   JEANIE TIETJEN

Deborah Pugh and Jeanie Tietjen met each other
and their students while teaching writing with the
WritersCorps program in Washington, D.C. Debbie
is a graduate of Longwood College and George
Mason University; she now lives in North Carolina.
Jeanie is a graduate of the University of Washington
at Seattle; she lives in Washington, D.C.

DATE			
1/98	(1)	11/97	